Wisdom as Moderation

SUNY Series in Philosophy
Robert C. Neville, Editor

Wisdom as Moderation

A Philosophy of the Middle Way

CHARLES HARTSHORNE

State University of New York Press

Published by
State University of New York Press, Albany

© 1987   State University of New York

For information, address State University of New York
Press, State University Plaza, Albany, N.Y., 12246

Library of Congress Cataloging-in-Publication Data

Hartshorne, Charles, 1897
    Wisdom as moderation.

    (SUNY series in philosophy)
    1. Philosophy.   I. Title.   II. Series.
B29.H345   1987   191   86-25657
ISBN 0-88706-472-8
ISBN 0-88706-473-6 (pbk.)

10 9 8 7 6 5 4 3 2 1

To D. C. H., from whom I am still learning how
to write better the language to which I was born

Contents

Acknowledgments

For permission to republish—in parts of this book as specified in brackets—the following essays, the author thanks the respective journals:

Phenomenology and Philosophical Research [Chapter five], "The Structure of Metaphysics: a Criticism of Lazerowitz's Theory," in vol. 19, 2 (Dec. 1958), 226–240. Also "How Some Speak yet Do Not Speak of God," in vol. 23, 2 (Dec., 1962), 274–78.

Wesleyan Studies in Religion [Chapter six], "Man's Fragmentariness," in vol. 41, 6 (1963–64), 17–28.

The Monist [Chapter seven], "Can Man Transcend His Animality?" in vol. 55, 2 (Apr., 1971), 208–217.

Theoria to Theory [Chapter eight], in vol. 13 (1079), 127–140. I thank the editor Dorothy Emmett for her request to write on the relation of my metaphysics to my ornithology and for permission to republish the article. The journal has been discontinued for financial reasons.

Chapter nine was published in a German Translation entitled "Rechte—nicht nur für Menschen" in *Zeitschrift für Evangelische Ethik*, 22, 1 (Jan., 1958).

Preface

Some years ago the idea expressed in the title of this book occurred to me, and much of Chapters One, Two, and Four were written then. More recently, when asked by the Lowell Foundation to give three lectures in Cambridge, Mass., I reworked Chapters One and Two and wrote Chapter Three to make a third lecture. Chapter Nine has been published only in a German translation. Chapter Ten was written recently for this book. The remaining four chapters are slightly revised or extended versions of essays published in various journals. Chapter Six was given as a lecture at West Virginia Wesleyan College.

The relation of the first three chapters to the title will be obvious. I leave it to the readers to decide how well the other chapters illustrate the same principle.

Chapter Seven would never have been written if the late Eugene Freeman, then editor of *The Monist*, had not chosen a similar title for an issue of his journal and asked me to contribute. This is only one of the ways in which I am indebted to this capable former student (one of the first graduate students I had the privilege of teaching).

This book, like my book on *Omnipotence*, is written for educated people in general, as well as for those trained in philosophy.

Students of Mahayana Buddhism will recognize the phrase 'middle way'. I have elsewhere explained why I think, with some support from T. I. Stcherbatski, that Buddhists did not quite succeed in their search for a mean between extreme eternalism and extreme temporalism, nor between extremes of monism and pluralism. But the time has gone past when it was altogether sufficient to ignore the efforts of the Orientals to achieve wisdom. Our western individualism, not adequately corrected by collectivism (and, yes, OUR materialism in several senses) now endanger all mankind and indeed life on earth. We are not so wise that we cannot learn from the great non-western traditions.

As the reader will discover, I have invented what seems a new way of referring to notes put at the end of the book, using letters for chapters and numbers for order within chapters. Thus 'A3' means the third note in Chapter One and C2 Means the second note in Chapter Three. The reader has the advantage of a single serial order for the whole book and the writer the advantage of not having to change all later numbers when he changes his mind about notes to add or eliminate. I have often as a reader been bothered by the trouble of locating the notes for a certain chapter each time one looks up a reference. My system solves that reading problem without making much trouble for the writer. A third advantage is it makes it easier to spot the numbers for notes in the text.

Though not the one to judge, I would not be astonished if some readers were to like this book at least as well as any other of my writings. Together with my *Creative Synthesis and Philosophic Method*, it deals with my various fundamental beliefs and theories as, in their most general aspects, forming a coherent metaphysics. Like the other book it gives some applications of the ideas to contingent, non-metaphysical topics. There is a vague agreement with Hegel ("The truth is the unity of contraries"), a closer one with Peirce and Whitehead, also with Bergson and, on theological issues, with Faustus Socinus ("the first Unitarian"), G. T. Fechner, Jules Lequier, and B. Varisco—yes and even with Plato as, following Cornford and Levinson, I interpret Plato. Because of these and many other historical reasons I call my form of metaphysics neoclassical. Only in this century could so many fundamental motifs of the great traditions, including Buddhism and some forms of Vedantism, be made into a lucid and consistent whole. If the lucidity and coherence are still not satisfactory, perhaps absolute success in this endeavor is only an ideal for our human mode of knowing, or for what Whitehead calls our "ape-like consciousness." But perhaps some of my readers can do it better. I have no doubt that some will try. My best wishes to them.

This is my last, or if I am lucky, my next to last philosophical book. In the last, already largely written, I try to make clearer in what sense neoclassical process philosophy is empirical, even though its metaphysical element is not; also in what sense it is in partial agreement with the results of phenomenology, existentialism, linguistic analysis, and hermeneutics in recent forms. Final decisions about this projected work will be made only after it has become clear what the contributions to *The Philosophy of Charles Hartshorne* (in the Library of Living Philosophers) and my replies to these will have left unsaid that I feel needs to be said, or what loose ends need tying tighter, such as the relation of metaphysics to formal logic and natural and social science.

The Mean and
the False Extremes

THE GOOD AS A MEAN

Starvation is not good, overeating is not good. Caution can go too far; so can boldness. Some persons are kind to friends but neglect their civic duties or obligations to strangers; some support good causes but are unkind to their personal associates. Well did Aristotle say that virtues in contrast to vices are judicious means between contrary extremes. But the principle holds much more generally than even Aristotle saw. It applies, for example, in aesthetic matters. Beauty, too, is a mean. It is not the opposite to ugliness. Ugliness is an incongruity, a disorder, a jolt; but the sheer absence of incongruity and disorder is not beauty. Rather, beauty and all aesthetic value is what, in the words of Kurt Sachs the musicologist, "lies between the fatal extremes of mechanism and chaos." By 'mechanism,' understand a too strict and unrelenting orderliness, and by 'chaos,' a sheer lack of order. In the first case there is too little surprise, sense of tension, or interest in how things may come out; in the second case there are no definite expectations to be met with pleased surprise or to awaken any desire to experience the outcome. With mechanism we are merely bored, with chaos merely confused. In neither way does the sense of beauty arise. Some marriages break up through boredom, a too complete orderliness, an excess of predictability; others, through intense conflicts and too little predictability. The great musicians use discords as well as harmonies. Satisfying persons must be partly predictable and partly unpredictable.

When works of art deviate from the mean of order-disorder toward the extreme of disorder, we may call them ugly, grotesque, and the like. When they deviate toward the extreme or order, we may call them tidy or 'neat' (as this word was used by the generation before the latest one), but not beautiful. At the limit of either direction of deviation from the mean, all aesthetic value lapses, and we turn to something else.

If aesthetic value were sheer harmony, why would people respond to advertisements of plays or cinemas proclaiming the shocking, even frightening, discords, conflicts, tensions, in these dramas? And people do respond. It is monotony that we shy away from, as much almost as danger or chaos. We want problems as well as solutions, the unexpected as well as the expected.

There is another way in which beauty is a mean. There are superficial and profound orders and disorders, harmonies and discords. "Superficial" means such that the resources of the person are not greatly called upon to appreciate the order or disorder. A simple musical chord is a superficial harmony, a Mozart symphony or Bach Chorale is a profound one. A little flower is like the simple chord; a well-designed flower garden or a natural forest is, by contrast, on the profound side. We may call the flower or the chord pretty, the symphony, or entire garden or forest, beautiful. Language thus nicely distinguishes superficial from profound harmonies. There are also superficial and profound discords. In Chopin's funeral march are some of the latter, for obvious reasons. Profound discords disrupting an expected or hoped-for harmony may be termed tragic, implying that we take them seriously, they challenge us to the depths. Superficial, unserious discords, similarly disrupting expectations, are comic; we may laugh at them or at least smile.

The foregoing aesthetic analysis can be summed up in a diagram. The vertical dimension is the contrast between extremes of order-disorder, or unity-variety, harmony-discord. Whether the harmony or lack of it is superficial or profound is expressed, not on this dimension; but on the horizontal one. Beauty, in the most natural sense of the word, is the center, the *double mean in both dimensions*. It is neither extraordinarily ununified, relative to the given variety, nor extraordinarily unified in the same reference, and it is neither extremely profound nor extremely superficial. A chord has both unity and variety, but on a superficial level, giving small challenge to our musical capacities. A symphony may have the same balance in its combination of unity and diversity as the chord, but vastly more diversity is effectively unified by it.

When the mean of order-disorder is profound, we are more likely to call a work sublime or magnificent than simply to term it beautiful. Is *The Winter's Tale* merely beautiful? It is more than that. *King Lear* even more obviously is sublimely tragic rather than simply beautiful or comic. And *The Merry Wives of Windsor* is comic rather than either beautiful or sublime.

It seems particularly instructive that comedy, beauty, tragedy, the sublime, the pretty, the neat or tidy, are all aesthetic terms in the same sense. They, or other qualities like them, are what we seek in art, literature, drama, music. They all have the status of values enjoyed for their own sakes. If we are thrilled by a beautiful thing, or amused by a comical one, we do not ask, of what use is the experience? Nor

Diagram of Aesthetic Values

Undiversified unity, absolute order

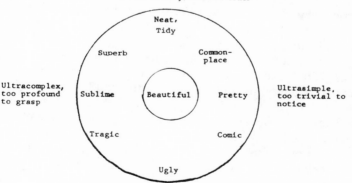

Ununified diversity, absolute disorder

Outside the circle no experience and no value, inside the circle some experience and some value.[A1]

do we ask this if we feel something to be sublime. These experiences are all good in themselves. And experiences good in themselves are the final topics of aesthetics when this subject is taken at its deepest. Would that this were more widely understood!

Morality is concerned with behavior whereby we make life in the long run more likely to furnish, for ourselves and others, experiences good in themselves. What gives experiences intrinsic value is a problem for the ultimate aesthetics, rather than for mere morality as such.

Many persons make a great fuss, for instance, about the sanctity of marriage but show little comprehension of what furthers intrinsic value in married life. Many talk about respect for life but seem unaware of the vast gulf in aesthetic quality between experiences open to a fetus (or even a newborn infant) compared to experiences possible for a walking, talking child, not to mention the more or less adult mother of the fetus or infant. Life on what level? that is the question. The single human egg cell is alive, and a wondrous thing, too, but it has no experiences such as you or I may have. And no egg cell, fertilized or not, can simply turn itself into a truly human individual. Only years of loving attention by others can do that. Without that loving attention the mere physical survival is no very good thing, by any criterion of value that science or philosophy is aware of. We need a golden mean in this *respect for life* business. But ideal moderation, judiciousness, is rare in the sense in which ideal virtue is rare. People get a thrill out of being injudicious. There would be some aesthetic loss in this sense if we were all ideally moderate. But there is also a price for the excesses. They make for bad laws, for one thing.

It is obvious that terms like "superficial," "unity in variety," "humorous" have a certain relativity to the individual having the experience. What taxes the resources of one person to appreciate may not tax the resources of another. Adults and children obviously differ in this respect, and education plays a role. But for each person there will be such contrasts as those between beautiful and merely pretty, or sublime and merely beautiful, or tragic and comic. And all of these express positive values. Even ugliness is not the sheer absence of aesthetic value. When we are confronted with what for us yields no intrinsic value at all, we have simply no experience. Absolute monotony cannot be experienced, nor can absolute chaos. Nothing in the world is in itself merely chaotic nor, according to a now common view in physics, is anything entirely ordered. And certainly no experience is merely ordered or merely chaotic.

THE GOLDEN MEAN IN METAPHYSICS

The idea of the judicious mean is applicable not only in ethics and aesthetics but also in speculative philosophy or metaphysics. It is, first of all, applicable to the very question whether or not there is a legitimate subject of metaphysics, in spite of the view, increasingly common since Hume and Kant, that the history of this undertaking is a history of pretentious nonsense. I do believe that this fashionable view is an injudicious extreme. The contrary extreme is an undue trust in some past or present achievements by metaphysicians.

Over and over again examination of the writings of the anti-metaphysicians reveals two things: first, they have a more or less unconscious metaphysics of their own which, for all they know, is as vulnerable as the metaphysics they attack, and second, and above all, the examples of metaphysics they choose for criticism are usually extremes of metaphysical doctrine, not the golden mean where the truth lies. Bradley's mystical monism is one of these extremes, and it has been a target of some critics of metaphysics as such. The radical pluralism his position implies. Nor does he really establish that it has most influential of recent anti-metaphysicians, Wittgenstein, after first adopting (or seeming to adopt) Russell's basic principle (essentially the pluralism of Hume in modern dress) later rejected it, but without ever telling us what mean between mere monism and mere pluralism has position implies. Nor does he really establish that it has no such implication. From the falsity of the two extremes mentioned, it does not follow that there is no truth lying between these extremes.

Much metaphysics has been bad, granted. How does it follow from this that there can be no good metaphysics? Good metaphysics means one that avoids the extremism that is the mark of error in philosophy and in life. It does not say, with pure monism, that all things are *interdependent* (and so indistinguishable from one another) or with pure pluralism that all things are *mutually independent* (and so with no real connections corresponding to our trust in causal inferences from one set of things or facts to others).

Wittgenstein held that metaphysicians habitually misuse language. It is not necessary to counter this statement with an extreme denial. Metaphysicians have often misused language; and so (for example, in their use of 'metaphysics') have some disciples of Wittgenstein. But to take the former fact as *defining* 'metaphysics' is an example of the use of "persuasive definitions." It has not been shown that linguistic care and responsibility are incompatible with belief in a third possibility over and above the extremes of metaphysical doctrine. A number of metaphysicians have tried, I hold with gradually increasing success, to clarify the "middle way," to use the Buddhist phrase, in metaphysical belief. But it is these metaphysicians that the critics of the subject usually ignore. Peirce and Whitehead, for example, are not extreme pluralists; moreover, they have thought deeply about the role of language in their subject.

THE PRINCIPLES OF CONTRAST AND POLARITY

Wittgenstein points out that metaphysicians sometimes fail to see or apply the "principle of contrast," according to which concepts must express contrast or lose their meaning, and that doctrines which eliminate one side of a contrast destroy the meaning of the other side.[A2] Hegel's metaphysics was built upon this very principle, and if the system was a failure this was partly because the principle was not consistently applied and partly for other reasons. Whitehead's system is also built upon the principle and avoids some at least of Hegel's extremisms.

The touchstones of preserving contrast and avoiding extremes come to much the same thing. Monism either denies plurality in favor of unity, or renders the plurality unitelligible by asserting universal interdependence and inseparability. Pluralism denies or renders unintelligible the connectedness of things to make a cosmos. Neither view does justice to the contrast between unity and plurality.

One contrast that must be preserved is that between actual and possible, or concrete and abstract. Mere nominalism, the denial of universals, makes language unintelligible; for words express universal aspects of things if they express anything. But the attempt to explain particulars as mere conjunctions of universals also fails. The contrast universal-particular must not be suppressed. The problem is to find the judicious mean between these denials.

The judicious mean can hardly be the mere togetherness of universals and particulars, just as the mean between monism and pluralism can hardly be the mere togetherness of unity and variety. Aristotle long ago declared that universal forms are in concrete actualities, not off by themselves. They are in us, for example, as concrete thinkers of the forms, and in events as concrete embodiments of forms. The Neoplatonists held that the forms are divine thoughts, and any theist will say something like this. But only recent metaphysics, so far as I can see, has found the right clue to the way the universal-particular contrast occurs in experience and reality. This clue is the temporal structure of experience when this is rightly understood. Experience exhibits a contrast, *one of the most basic of contrasts, between the actualized happenings of the past and the possible or probable but not actual happenings of the future.* Particulars are all past; *there are no future particulars.* To think the future is to think in more or less general terms; for there is no other way to think "future events." The becoming of events is the particularization of more or less general plans, purposes, tendencies, potentialities. There is no such thing as a fully particularized plan, purpose, or potentiality. Always much is left for the future to further define or determine. The very meaning of plan or purpose implies this. Futurity and generality are two aspects of the same basic mode of reality. How few are the logicians or metaphysicians who have clearly seen this! Aristotle, great logician, seemed to see it. Did Plato see it? Probably, to some extent. Do most logicians see it today? I gather that they do not. But Peirce (and his disciple W. P. Montague) saw it, and Whitehead saw it. James, Dewey, and Bergson all with some clarity saw it.

A nominalism that limits reality to particulars is really attempting to do away with the future as we experience it. The opposite form of "nominalism," limiting reality to the universal, is attempting to do away with the past.[A3] Either way the modal contrast which is essential to becoming is destroyed. *The ultimate universal is creativity, becoming, as particularized only in its past products, and as open to further particularization as new events are created.*

Where have the critics of metaphysics carefully discussed this kind of doctrine? I repeat, where?

Fully worked out, the principle of contrast, when applied to ideas of metaphysical generality, turns into something like Morris Cohen's "Principle of Polarity."[A4] If there can be a particular color, say green, in the absence of its opposite, red, this is because the various colors are special cases of the more general idea of color, and of the still more general idea of sensory quality. But metaphysical terms like universal-particular, or cause-effect, are too general to be treated as mere special cases. Particular entities have universal aspects; every effect becomes a cause and there are no causes not productive of subsequent effects. Both sides of metaphysical contrasts must be illustrated in every actual case. This principle of Morris Cohen's is of great value in discriminating good from bad metaphysics. It is particularly important in philosophy of religion. God is not merely infinite or merely finite; merely absolute or merely relative; merely immutable or merely mutable. Deity is rather the supreme synthesis of these contraries.

DETERMINISM AND MATERIALISM AS EXTREMES

In some cases the difficulty in finding the golden mean of doctrine arises partly from the fact that one of the two extremes is so obviously untenable that by comparison the opposite extreme appears imperative. Philosophers in logic classes teach that contraries cannot both be true but may both be false, yet in doing or discussing metaphysics they tend to forget this. Example: the contrary extreme to strict or unqualified causal determinism (certainly an extreme doctrine if there is one) is sheer unqualified causal indeterminism, implying that in any situation, say S, anything that could conceivably occur in any other situation could with equal probability occure in S. No animal could adapt itself to the world on such a basis. So this extreme no one defends. By astonishing lack of caution the opposite extreme has been blandly asserted by countless philosophers. Nothing has more sharply distinguished metaphysics since about 1880, and increasingly until today, from that in the 17th-to-early-19th-centuries, than the realization that this early modern procedure has been thoroughly uncritical. Sheer causal chaos or disorder is totally unbelievalble, so much all can see. Unqualified causal determinism or absolute order is not so crudely incredible, yet on careful examination it has by many philosophers and scientists been judged equally erroneous. It ignores the contrast without which 'order' is meaningless. It destroys 'time's arrow,' and violates the conditions for understanding the universal-particular or possible-actual distinction.

Strawson, like many others, tells us that there can be no metaphysical or a priori support for empirical knowledge since "chaos is conceivable." The quoted assertion is metaphysical; taken without qualification it is a questionable extreme akin to Hume's axiom that any two distinguishable events must also be separable events, that is: either's occurrence is logically independent of the other's occurrence, and no relations among events can be internal to or constitutive of any of the events. This is one extreme of metaphysical doctrine of which the contrary extreme is that no relations among events can be *ex*ternal to or *non*constitutive of any of the events.

In spite of Hume it is self-evident that events can be distinguishable without being unqualifiedly separable. What happens during a given hour is distinguishable from what happens during the first half of the hour; but whereas the stretch of happenings during the whole hour includes or logically implies what happens during the first half hour, the converse implication obtains only if determinism is taken as logically true. This is only the most obvious and trivial counterexample to Hume's dictum, which is one of the most illustrious instances of bad metaphysics.

I hold, with a number of other philosophers, that neither pure disorder nor pure, unqualified order could be real, or is genuinely conceivable as a possible state of affairs. In either case human or animal decisions generally would be meaningless. The task of induction (or—*pace* Popper—of empirical inquiry) is not to adjudicate between the extremes of order-disorder; for the whole import of induction and rational decision is that both extremes are excluded. It could never be rational to arrive by induction at the conclusion that induction is impossible, since there is no order in events. It also could never be rational to arrive in this way, or any other way, at the conclusion that the future is uniquely implied by the causal past. For the function of causal knowledge cannot be to make our choices for us by eliminating all possibilities but one; rather, the function is to indicate the really open possibilities (compatible with the causal past) so that we may make a choice among these possibilities.

The metaphysical contribution to the induction problem is the modest one of making clear that the forward aspect of becoming can only be a mean between a wholly closed and a wholly open future. Where this mean lies it is the task of science to discover. Current physics (with its probabilistic or statistical ideal of laws) comes closer to fulfilling this task than classical physics, which appeared to support the monistic extreme of total interdependence. That the extremes of independence and interdependence are absurdities follows from the metaphysical axiom of contrast. Dependence and independence must both be real if either is to make sense, and no induction is needed to establish this. In their treatment of this problem Hume and Bradley are equally, though in opposite ways, proponents of the absurd. In the West, it is easier to see the absurdity of sheer monism; in Asia the absurdity of sheer pluralism.

How far the qualified causal orderliness that must obtain makes it practically possible for a given type of animal to learn by experience sufficiently to survive, or to arrive at science such as we have and eventually to better science than we have, is a more specific matter than the question of there being some causal order to know. All life requires some degree of trust in a usable natural order. Metaphysics does not guarantee that induction will lead us to the exact truth, nor that it will enable us to dispense with great effort in moving toward the approximate truth. We remain dependent upon the continuing exertions of scientists, some with genius and many with competence, to gradually bring us closer to a correct picture of our cosmos.

Another difficult case is that of materialism and its apparent contrary, idealism. Is not the contrast of mind to matter one that must be preserved? Must we not recognize both poles of this contrast as genuine? I reply, "Yes indeed," but what is the contrast? "Mind" taken in its most generic meaning refers to processes of experiencing, remembering, feeling, desiring, deciding and the like. These are positive ideas. "Matter," as Descartes saw so well, has the positive properties of spatial location, locomotion, and shape or configuration. A judicious philosophy will not deny the reality of whatever has these properties. Dualism arises only when we suppose, as Descartes did, that what thinks or feels cannot have location, locomotion, or configuration, and that what has the latter, the spatial properties, cannot think or feel. Neither of these negations is self-evident. For all that anyone has demonstrated, the same realities that think or feel also have spatial properties. Indeed unless both sets of properties were in our experiences we should not know anything about them, or have any idea of them. And whatever thinks or feels is what we mean by "mind," whether or not it has the spatial properties. So some form of idealism remains a tenable doctrine.

But, you may argue, surely we do in common sense contrast mind and body, mental states and material things or events. Tables and planets, trees and crystals, seem rather obviously unthinking and insentient entities. I admit the reality of the contrast between thinking or sentient "things" and unthinking insentient ones. This contrast must be preserved. However, Leibniz showed once and for all that neither materialism nor even dualism in the metaphysical sense is entailed by the contrast. The population of a city, taken as one thing, does not literally think or feel; only its individual members do this. Analogously the population, or immense group, of molecules making up a table or a planet, or probably even the colony of cells and their corpses making up a tree, do not think or feel, but nevertheless individual atoms, molecules, or cells may, if not think, at least feel in some minimal fashion. So the common sense contrast between sentient and insentient can be preserved without any ultimate dualism, much less any sheer materialism. Science has shown to be illusory or at least problematic the common sense criteria (e.g., inertness, lack of responsiveness to environment) for the total absence of sentience in parts of nature; materialists or dualists have yet to show that there are any other valid criteria. Leibniz's arguments (or Peirce's or Whitehead's) for psychicalism have not been refuted.

The criterion of no nervous system for the insentient is merely question begging. Such a system is the way a colony of cells (in the human body hundreds of billions of them) acquires the dynamic unity that a single cell or protozoön has without such a system. The network of nerves restores on a more complex level the ability to *act-as-one* which single cells and molecules have on their own. This ability is the external evidence of feeling, and its absence is the only cogent evidence of lack of feeling. In addition, when we feel pain we directly intuit cellular feeling—this being the most straightforward possible explanation of how we derive feeling qualities from cellular injuries. Thus feeling on a radically subhuman level is, for all anyone has shown, a positive datum, not a mere hypothesis; its denial *is* such an hypothesis, and a purely negative one at that. A materialist employs question-begging criteria for "no feeling anywhere here." Now that science has established the illusoriness of the common sense criteria for "mere matter" (except as showing the insentience of certain aggregates of individual entities), philosophers might at long last catch up with Leibniz. By this I do not mean accepting his monadology as it stands. For that doctrine is a mixture of doctrines, not a single doctrine.

Regarding the place of mind in reality there are two opposite absurdities: the idea of a total absence of mind in large portions of nature, a psychical zero or vacuum; and the idea of an absolute psychical maximum, a supreme mind or supermind containing as actual all possible positive qualities and values. On the contrary, some of us believe, there could not be any psychically vacuous portions of nature and there could not be an exhaustive realization of all possible psychical values. The ground for becoming (in all actuality, even divine) is precisely this; that potentialities for experiencing or feeling form an open infinity with no upper limit. No matter what value is actual, there could and should and will be more. Likewise, what makes being or becoming pervasively intelligible is that there is no lower limit of such potentialities, no zero or absolute minimum of the psychical except the zero of reality itself. Leibniz showed himself a mathematician when he remarked in this context that between any finite quantity and zero there can be an infinite number of fractions. Human experiencing and value may sometimes seem a small thing; but there is still much room below it short of no experiencing, no sentience, no value, at all. There is room for all the animals, single cells, molecules, atoms, and particles.

The force of the foregoing reasoning is beginning to be seen by quite a number of physicists and biologists.[A5] Leibniz, Peirce, and Whitehead were, let us remember, all physicists.

Psychicalism and materialism are not contrary impossibilities, like extreme monism and extreme pluralism. Whereas the significance of unity depends upon its contrast with diversity, that of mind does not depend upon its contrast with mere mind-and-value-empty matter. Mind requires objects known, but since other minds can be known they can fulfill this requirement. And the principle of contrast is further fulfilled by the admission of aggregates which are not (single) minds and do not think or feel. Also, abstract objects do not think or feel. Finally there is contrast between high and low levels of feeling or thinking. Thus belief in the golden mean and the imperative of contrast is compatible with psychicalism.

Sheer materialism is an extreme of doctrine that has always been a minority position. (I am not forgetting communism.) But dualism has often seemed, and been taken perhaps by majorities, as a mean between the psychicalistic and physicalistic extremes. However, to assert "both-and" is not always the right way to do justice to two contrasting conceptions. It may be a way of missing what is wrong with both of the extremes. The idea of mere nonspatialized, non-physical mind is as erroneous as the idea of mere, wholly non-psychical matter. If all extended things have a psychical aspect and all sentient individuals an extended aspect, then dualism doubly misses the truth. It is a false compromise.[A6]

Nor is the traditional Spinozistic two-aspect theory of reality the true mean. For the psychical aspect is the concrete or inclusive one and the other is abstract by comparison. Merely *where* something is, how its parts are *arranged* (giving the thing its shape), how *fast* it is changing its locus, how its locational changes *influence* similar changes in its neighbors, these are very partial descriptions of a thing. It is such changes that physics informs us about. What is omitted is quality in the distinctive sense in which yellow, sour, pain, pleasure, love, hate, hope, fear, are qualitative; but shape and velocity are not. Spinoza's "thought" and "extension" are not coordinate; for the second term is radically abstract, compared to the other. Leibniz saw this, Spinoza and many since of Spinoza have not seen it.

CHAPTER TWO (B)

Moderation in Theory of Knowledge and Philosophy of Religion

THE OPPOSITE ERRORS OF RATIONALISM AND EMPIRICISM

By "rationalism" as an error I mean precisely what Brand Blanshard neatly expressed by the dictum: "To understand is to see to be necessary." Spinoza believed this; Bosanquet, Bradley, and (with some quibbling) Royce imply it; Leibniz's principle of sufficient reason is only by sophistries distinguished from it.[B1] By "empiricism" as an error I mean the opposite doctrine, "To understand is to see to be contingent," except that, since scarcely anyone wants to say that arithmetic is only contingently true, in practice empiricism is the doctrine that to understand *existential* statements (where to exist means more than to have a necessary place in some conceptual system) is to see them not to be necessary. This was the view of Hume and his innumerable disciples, with some support from Kant.

I hold, against empiricism, that Anselm discovered the noncontingency of any high form of theism. He did not prove theism to be necessarily true, but he established the dilemma: it is *either* necessarily true *or* necessarily untrue (contradictory or absurd). Aristotle had already implied this; as, I believe, and not I alone, had Plato.

15

(Nothing eternal can be contingent. Accidents do not happen in eternity.) In addition "something exists" is noncontingently true, for the 'being of total nonbeing' is either nonsense or contradiction. Here, too, I am far from the first to say so.

Rationalism as Blanshard defines it has been rejected by any number of thinkers, including three of the great logicians, Aristotle, Peirce, and Whitehead. The principle of contrast is unfavorable to either of the two onesided doctrines considered in this section. As always, however, the principle applies in *nonsymmetrical* fashion to the two extremes. As the concrete includes the abstract (Aristotle), so an empirical truth always has a nonempirical aspect. The metaphysical necessities, which are very abstract, are everywhere and always (however unobviously) instantiated. That I exist is contingent; but it follows necessarily from this that either I have a relation of dependence to God (assuming the divine existence is not impossible) or that I do not have such a relation (if the divine existence is impossible). Note that the necessity of my relation to God (or the necessary absence of God) is conditional on my existing. Indispensable for me, the relation is not indispensable for God, who exists no matter what (unless the theistic idea is logically impossible).

Popper's definition of "empirical" (that it implies *some conceivable experiences would falsify*, and some would at least be compatible with, what is asserted) fits the moderate view I am presenting. Note that, while any empirical truth will illustrate also some purely rational or metaphysical truth, no purely rational or necessary truth will illustrate any empirical or contingent truth. The fact that the rational truth is stated by a given individual in a given way and language will exemplify empirical truth; but the truth stated, say that $2 + 3 = 5$, will not do so. Necessary truth is astract, in a sense empty; no concrete truth is necessary. 'God exists', if true, is in some ways as abstract a truth as can well be stated; for it implies nothing about what else exists, apart from the extremely abstract truth that *something* else must also exist, some divinely inspired and sustained world or other. Not even the laws of this "some world" are deducible.

A difficult question arises about the status of phenomenology as a method not perhaps classifiable under either of the two extremes mentioned. Husserl certainly recognized both contingent and necessary aspects of reality. So did Peirce in his phaneroscopy or phenomenology. I believe that Peirce's doctrines of Firstness,

Secondness, and Thirdness, with some revisions, are indeed nonempirical truths that any conceivable experience would illustrate and none would falsify. But Secondness is scarcely detectible in Husserl's account; and this is enough to make me prefer the Peircean account. None of the three ideas is clear unless all are. Heidegger's account, in my judgment, lacks the clarity of either Husserl or Peirce. The truth I recognize in Heidegger seems, much of it, better stated by others.

The pragmatic criterion of meaning applies to statements of either class, but suffices to establish truth as well meaning only in metaphysical or purely rational issues. I have argued this in two writings.[B2]

Two Extreme and Two Moderate Views of Genetic Identity

In this section I will illustrate several of the working principles that I find helpful in metaphysics. One is the principle expressed in the title of this book. Another is the use of the history of ideas for the resources it furnishes for solving our present problems. A third is the method of systematic exhaustion of theoretical options in solving a problem.

In dealing with the question, "What is meant by saying that a changing thing or person is the *same* through its changes?" I feel that I have benefited by discussions with Paul Weiss, Andrew Reck, and I. M. Bochenski. This came about as follows. Weiss kept insisting that my Whiteheadian or Buddhist view of self-identity makes it impossible to understand obligation incurred by past actions; Reck charged me with insufficient appreciation of Aristotle's view on the subject, and Bochenski remarked that Aristotle's view of individual substances was essentially compatible with the modern doctrine that reality consists of "events not things," although Aristotle "did not dot all the i's and cross all the t's." Together the three contemporaries forced me to keep thinking about the relations between my view and traditional views until I reached as high a level of clarity as I can on this topic. I believe I now see some of the uncrossed t's and undotted i's.

As usual, the history of ideas provides us with the extremes between which any moderate view must be found. Hume states the negative extreme: there is simply *no* identity between earlier and later states of a changing person or thing, there is at most only similarity. Leibniz had already favored the world with the precisely opposite extreme: there is *complete* identity. The successive states of course differ, but yet *in each state* is the totality of states forward and backward in time. "The law of succession" of the states is immanent in each state. For instance, I have always been the one who "was going" to write this sentence. How could there be more identity than that, and yet change?

Aristotle clearly held a view other than either of the two extremes. In every state there are accidental qualities not essential to the individual's being that individual, yet in some real sense there is also identity. I hold that all sensible people are with Aristotle here. Hume and Leibniz are both wrong. So far I see Weiss and Reck as with Aristotle. But so is Whitehead. His personally-ordered societies have more than similarities relating later to earlier states; each state prehends, and in this sense possesses as immanent constituents, the *earlier* states. So far Whitehead is with Leibniz and against Hume. But concerning the future, Whitehead is rather far from both Hume and Leibniz and not far from Aristotle, agreeing with him that the future is only potential and somewhat indeterminate. What then is the remaining difference?

Whitehead sees clearly and Aristotle somewhat fails to see that to have a predicate accidentally is, for the subject, not really to "have" the predicate in the same sense as it has the predicates that constitute its identity. If I was already "myself" in childhood, still *that* self did not have and never can have my adult knowledge. The adult in its memories has its childhood, but no child can have its adulthood. As Leibniz saw, and Whitehead agrees, the tradition was playing fast and loose with the term identity. There is partial identity, yes; but no complete identity between a child and any adult. Simply unqualified identity, simply unqualified nonidentity, are both errors, for which two modern men of genius made themselves severally responsible. We can therefore more readily see what views cannot be correct.

The fully determinate units of reality are momentary actualities that "become but do not change." They are created and henceforth indestructible. Retrospectively, or by prehending, they have their past in their present, but not their futures, which as definite actualities do not exist.

What kept Aristotle from seeing as clearly as Whitehead or the Buddhists that the identity of an individual cannot, in a simple, directionless sense, include its successive states, and that the full self of the moment is new with that moment? Part of the explanation is in Aristotle's belief that experiencing is *continuous*. A continuum has no least or singular unit-parts, unless points or instants, and of these there would be an infinity in any portion, however short. Such an infinity of units is as good as no units at all. We could never come even close to one and hence can find no definite terms for relations of succession. So the units of reality must, it was thought, be individuals, throughout their careers simply the same units. Hence many a paradox in Aristotelianism. Before Whitehead, all over the world, most thinkers (apart from Buddhists) were involved in this difficulty. William James, with his "buds" or "drops" of experiencing, taken up by Whitehead, combined with quantum physics, and his knowledge of Zeno's paradoxes jogged Whitehead into a clear acceptance of the "epochal" view of becoming. He also had partly the same ethico-religious reasons as the Buddhists for valuing the pluralization of "substances" into momentary actualities. For prehension, which gives one a partial identity with one's own past selves, gives one also a less intimate partial identity with the past selves of other neighboring individuals or personally-ordered societies. Inheritance by prehension is the principle in both cases.

History shows us with significant clarity what happens when people believe that the final units of reality are individuals. "I am I and you are you; do I care about myself? Of course, for I am myself. Do I care about you? Oh, that is a problem. You are not I." Derivation of altruism from enlightened self-interest is the next step. Weiss's own ethics is on a higher level. But then, why does he not see that it is the exaggeration both of self-identity and of nonidentity between selves that stands between people and that higher level? Do young persons really wholly identify themselves with the elderly persons they may eventually become? Sympathy with one's remote future self is not automatic; and the notion that self-interest is rational and interest in others is so only by the detour of enlightened self-interest has seemed to me for all my adult life a strange notion of rationality. What needs to be enlightened is not *self*-interest, but simply interest in, concern for, those selves with which we have to do and which we can influence or help—as the Scriptures have it, ourselves and our neighbors. The great saying, "We are members one of another" is good Buddhism and good Whiteheadianism. "Love thy neighbor *and thyself*," taken seriously, implies the same ideal.

How about remorse for past wrongdoing? One is still, in part, that previous self, and this may, in the case in hand, be the relevant part of one's present self. Absolutes will not help in these matters. "I am simply not that self"; "I simply am that self"; these are both wrong. One should not try to dissect with an axe, as Peirce liked to say. That on the issue before us Peirce was on the Buddhist side is a textually defensible claim. What held him back from clarity on this topic is no mystery: it was his extreme continuitism or "synechism." This was a false extreme that said: the conceivably possible is continuous [true]; the actual also is continuous [false, unless carefully qualified]. On this issue Peirce was an extremist, as was his brilliant father.

THE FASCINATION OF EXTREME VIEWS: MATERIALISM AGAIN

Where extreme clashes with contrary extreme there is often, on both sides, a conviction (perhaps not wholly conscious) of the impossibility of a middle position. In 'mind and matter' the 'and' hides the real problems, according to the partisans of mind as well as the partisans of matter. Here I think both are right. But there are extremist views of mind as well as of matter; and the rejection of dualism does not of itself tell us which of the two concepts has the unlimited scope that entitles it to interpret all reality. This surely cannot obtain of 'mind' *if* that means something closely similar to the feeling and thinking found in adult human beings, or in human beings and God, as in Bishop Berkeley's theory. If by 'matter' one merely denotes whatever it is that is studied in physics, biology, and psychology as going on in us and our environment, or in the spatio-temporal whole, then, apart from deity, this is indeed the universal reality. But the question, "What makes it matter *rather than mind*?" is still unanswered. Human thinking and feeling are surely going on in space-time, for all anyone can show. And the Leibnizian distinction between singular and aggregate takes care of the lack of analogy between us and stones or planets, or even between us and trees, without necessarily giving any support to the alleged concept of mere dead, insentient matter, devoid as a whole *and in its parts* of anything like sensing, feeling, or thinking.

What is the appeal of materialism? Like idealism it avoids a mere *and* connecting mind and matter. In addition it invites us to dismiss such questions as, "What does it feel like to be an atom, or a cell, or perhaps even a fish?" And since most scientists do not ask such questions (unless a few psychologists in the last two cases), dismissing them may seem reasonable. The intellectual scene is simplified therewith. Is simplicity a sign of truth? Mario Bunge, a materialist, derides the claim that it is in his *Myth of Simplicity*. His view here is rather extreme; but this does not mean that the contrary extreme would be sound.

Without a search for unification of concepts under more general concepts, we should have no science. We *must* "seek simplicity," even though, as Whitehead adds, we should also "distrust it." Moreover, there is ambiguity in the simplicity of materialism. If in some bits of matter there is, neither in whole nor in part, any analogy to what in us is called feeling, memory, purpose, or thought, then is not materialism really an emergent dualism? Wholly unfeeling stuff or process becomes stuff with feeling and the like. The great psychicalists, from Leibniz to Peirce and Whitehead, treat the psychical not as an addition to mere matter, but as, in its possible varieties, the whole of what matter is, even in its most primitive forms (atoms or particles). These thinkers analyze even the extendedness of things in space in psychical terms. Thus their idealism can claim to be the only real overcoming of dualism. The concept of matter, they hold, is dispensable if the concept of mind is sufficiently generalized. As for the claim that the concept of matter, equally generalized, also covers the whole ground, since this matter, as in us, feels and thinks, and since there seems to be no nonquestion-begging criterion of mere, insentient matter (insentient in its parts and as a whole), how is it to be known that the materialists' matter is anything but an inadequate view of what the psychicalist calls mind?

The least ambiguous implication of materialism is negative: that to arrive at an idea of concrete reality in its *universal* traits we need not consider our experiences, feelings, or thoughts, as such, at all. "What is it to be concretely real? Well, take an atom as physics deals with it." This assumes that we know what it is like concretely to be an atom. But surely what we know is what it is like to observe experimental results in dealing with things understandable as composed of atoms. By immediate memory (or, as some of us think, the same thing, "introspection"), we know directly what it is like to feel, sense, or remember. Must not, in last analysis, our idea of reality be derived by analogical generalization from such direct awareness rather than from our rather indirect and highly abstract knowledge of atoms? However this may be, it seems manifest that materialism, *in its least ambiguous aspect*, forbids us to put such questions as, "How do atoms or particles feel?" It *bars the path of inquiry* to this extent. Materialism, and dualism as well, limits, intellectual inquiry. We have to talk about mind as such; we do not have to talk about matter as mindless.

Psychicalism puts no limit on inquiry, unless one can find a non-question-begging criterion for the total absence of feeling or sentience in parts of nature. And what would this criterion be? The physicists make no claim to possess it. And about the only psychologists that have with any care or seriousness considered the question have been psychicalists (Troland, Spearman, Wundt, Fechner, and at least a few others). The conclusion I draw is that the simplicity of materialism is specious. It simplifies our task by arbitrarily limiting our curiosity. It adds nothing positive to psychicalism, but only the negation, 'totally insentient stuff or process.'

Sometimes there seems almost a conspiracy among extremists to see to it that moderate positions should be ignored. There was a time, (I was then a Harvard student) when Anglo-American philosophical controversy seemed little more than a choice between "absolute idealism," meaning a fairly extreme monism (Royce, Bradley, Bosanquet, and others) and "realism," meaning a fairly extreme pluralism (Russell, Moore, and the American "new Realists" Perry, Spalding, and others). The pragmatists, especially Dewey, had a less extreme position but tended to present this position in rather loose, indefinite, or ambiguous terms. The "logical positivists" in their ontology (so far as they had one) were really Humean pluralists and not moderate at all. Then came linguistic analysts, culminating in the view that since we philosophize and do science through language, we are in a linguocentric predicament. We do not know God or nature but only talk about God or nature. This is a new form of anthropocentrism or anthropomorphism. It is one more extreme. In a sense it is an old extreme. Advaitist-vedantist Hindus and early Mahayana Buddhists held that what really matters in our view of life transcends what can be literally said and can only be attained by meditation that, in fortunate cases, enables us to experience the truth, although only those who have enjoyed similar experiences will be able to appreciate what we have found.

Is there not something amiss in saying that we do not know God (or nature) but only talk about God (or nature)? Is it only the *word* God (or nature) our talk is about? Some words do refer to words, for example 'word'. But many words have a different function from that of calling attention to language. Our eyes, ears, and senses of pain and pleasure are giving us experience of a great deal besides spoken or written words, or even gestures functioning along with words to communicate. There must be room for both a contrary extreme and a median position in this matter of language as a veil between us and other forms of reality.

Our human linguistic consciousness is an extension of animal awareness, such as infants, before learning words, may be supposed to almost share with many non-human animals. In some sense these creatures feel and in a primitive way perhaps think their bodily and environmental conditions. If theism has any truth, there is a third kind of awareness, which is above, as an infant's or a non-human animal's is below, the linguistic level. For neoclassical theism God feels and consciously knows how each creature feels, without having to verbalize this feeling or knowing. Our need for words is partly to enable us to deal selectively with the vast portions of reality we do not distinctly perceive or remember at a given moment. God does not need language for this purpose since divine perception and memory are inclusive and distinct. But God feels all our linguistic experiences and in that way possesses all human languages and their employments. God experiences our experiences or feelings distinctly *as* ours, analogously to our indistinct feeling of cellular feelings in our bodies. Hurt my cells, certain of them, and you hurt me. Hurt me and you hurt God. By the Platonic analogy, thus modernized, the old heresy of suffering deity makes sense.

We need language also to communicate with and influence others outside our bodies. God's eminent influencing of us is analogous to our influencing members of our bodies, and in both cases the influencing is more direct than the use of verbal signs. On our lower level we feel God's feelings as divinely made relevant to us; our cells on their still lower level feel something of our feelings. In such ways it seems to me that our linguistic thinking can give us some idea of the two nonhuman types of awareness, the one not needing or having language and the other needing and having it only as creatures using language are among its objects, while in eminent, inclusive fashion it enjoys-suffers-intuits the world. Somewhat as our cells' awareness of our experiences must be radically inadequate, so—and more so—must our sense of divine experiences be inadequate. That only some of us are consciously theists (and some think they are atheists) is therefore not altogether surprising.

In pragmatism there is an extreme illustrated by C. I. Lewis, my Harvard teacher (the one from whom I took more courses than from anyone else). He insisted to me that physical things, apart from living organisms, are merely there to be used, have no intrinsic life, awareness, or value. There is no room for sympathy or empathy, for attributing to them the least sentience, however primitive, slight, or trifling. Our fellow human beings, perhaps other animals, we can try to empathize with, but not with atoms or molecules. (What he thought about cells I do not know. My guess is he would have been less dogmatic on that question.) It is obvious that the idea of an absolutely insentient reality, neither as a whole nor in its constituents enjoying any feeling or thought, is a negative extreme. If God is thought of as the (in every respect) unsurpassable fullness of life, awareness, and value, then that is the opposite extreme.

According to process theology, whether in Whitehead's or my neoclassical form, even the divine extreme is not unqualifiedly so. Divine fullness of life is unsurpassable by others than God; but God, as Fechner held a century before, and more explicitly than, Whitehead, in richness of content is self-surpassing. There is growth even in the positive extreme. The negative extreme also needs qualifying. The zero of life and intrinsic value is a mere limiting concept. All actuality is better than that zero. Where there is no good at all there is no actuality at all. Between the extremes of divinity and the least actual creature there are the intermediate cases of high grade animality such as our human form. On other planets outside our solar system who knows what there may be? Is this an extreme doctrine? I submit it is a moderate doctrine, rejecting precisely the verbally possible extremes at both "ends" of the comparisons.

Lewis was a pragmatist and an admirer of Dewey. From a somewhat narrow pragmatic perspective they were both right in their idea of the merely instrumental value of inanimate objects. It is indeed idle to try to empathize with a mountain, and probably even with a tree. And for most human purposes individual atoms, molecules, or cells do not matter, taken one by one. We cannot stop to wonder what their feelings may be when deciding to use physical objects. We are ill equipped to know their values, taken individually, and we have no reason to think them comparable in intensity or richness to those of animals.

But, unlike the other animals, we human beings have interests transcending the merely practical in the narrow sense Dewey and Lewis had in mind. It is also, I think, significant, that Lewis not only refused to admit the possibility that inanimate nature has its own forms of life, experience, and value, but insisted also, concerning even other human beings, that the idea of their having, like ourselves, feelings and thought is only a (reasonable and practically needful) "postulate." What we *know* is only the others' behavior. This rejection of social knowledge as knowledge I take as a symptom of an extremist tendency, just as I take as extremist Lewis's *absolute* denial of any respectable reason to postulate sentience in the microconstituents of large portions of nature.

Lewis seems to have overlooked the critical question of our relations to our own bodily cells, with which we must somehow be directly related in our sensory experiences. Here is the test case for the basically social structure of experience and reality. For here the macroscopic and microscopic are together, with nothing between. The fact is that, under a wide range of circumstances, the rule obtains: hurt my cells and you hurt me, cause me pain, suffering; under other circumstances, what happens in my cells gives me pleasure, feelings opposite to pain. The simplest explanation of how this can be is that in such circumstances some of my cells themselves suffer or enjoy what is happening in them, and my pain or pleasure is my participation in theirs—with the difference that they are many and I at the moment am the one unified experience, and that my experience is on a vastly higher level. Also my pain or pleasure as mine is a "subjective form" of feeling (in Whitehead's language) and theirs as felt by me is an "objective form." This duality is inherent in the sympathetic or social structure of feeling as feeling of (other subjects' feelings.

With the one three-word phrase, "feeling *of* feeling," as he used it for his single term prehension, Whitehead inaugurated a new epoch in the intellectual history of mankind. That it has been left for me to say this in so many words is a sign of how novel this usage was. Most philosophers still do not see what it means. After twenty-five centuries of talk about divine love, implying that sympathy is the key to the coherence of the world, a philosopher actually says what, leaning on Whitehead, I have just said. Without Whitehead's help I was virtually saying it as a student at Harvard before Whitehead went there; but it took Whitehead to show how much could be done with the idea.

THE MIDDLE WAY IN PHILOSOPHY OF RELIGION

In regard to questions about God, what are the extremes? One extreme is atheism, the denial that there is any radically pre-eminent being. This implies that all individuals or realities are more or less like us in being without perfection in any strict sense. The opposite extreme is the assertion of a pre-eminent and *in all respects* perfect reality, perfection being conceived as an exhaustive actualization of *all* possible good properties. As the nontheistic extreme holds that only imperfect beings exist, the theistic extreme holds at least by implication (as we are about to see), that only perfect being or value exists. In the first case there is no definite standard or measure of degrees of value; in the second there are no degrees to measure, but only perfection itself. This crude outline may be clarified as follows:

Many theologians have said, in effect, that all possible value is actual in God, no matter what else exists. Then, if divine valuation is the measure of value, the creatures by this measure have simply no value, since by existing they add nothing to God's eternal value. This is an extreme way of exalting deity—by degrading the creatures to mere nothings. This becomes explicit in some forms of Vedantism. Another aspect of the same extremism is the claim that God's ideal power determines all that happens, the creatures merely carrying out their divinely preprogrammed destinies. Thus God's power is the only genuine power; the creatures are powerless. Again God is exalted by degrading the creatures. How could such mere puppets even conceive power in the genuine sense attributed to deity? The sad thing is that atheistic criticisms of theism as unable to solve the problem of evil argue from the extremist version of divine power as a monopoly. Thus theologians have madee things easy for atheists!

At the opposite extreme, nontheistic philosophies by implication unduly exalt the creatures by attributing to them not simply genuine power (and genuine value) but powers such as God alone is supposed by theists to possess, e.g., that of maintaining an orderly cosmos, or of measuring degrees of value so that it makes sense to say, for instance, that we human animals are "of more value than many sparrows," or of giving to the lives of mortal beings enduring significance not to be canceled out by death, including the death that must always remain a not to be excluded possibility for the future, that of the human species itself. I hold that atheism is excessive trust in the creatures—in animals, plants, stars, and their microconstituents. There is a mean between denying cosmic Power and Perfection (in some sense) and denying the genuineness of ordinary localized or imperfect forms of power and value.

The Buddhists are instructive cases in this regard. They seem not to be theists; but what miraculous powers and virtues they attribute to Buddha an the Bodhisattvas! One never knows where the line is between Buddha and divinity. How else can one read the Sutras? And what is Nirvana? There is a mean between so praising deity that it crowds out the creatures, and so praising the creatures that their need for deity is concealed by ambiguities or even perhaps stark nonsense. This is also illustrated by Jainism, and by some Western forms of humanism.

If the preservation of contrast is the touchstone, consider what contrasts are collapsed by nontheistic philosophies. God, say most theists, exists eternally and without possibility of not existing; other beings are contingent, their nonexistence was possible. This need not mean, and some of us believe should not mean, that there might have been nothing but God. I might not have existed, the earth might not have, and so on for every other definite thing other than God. It does not follow that God might have been alone. It may be that the supreme creative power was bound to produce some world or other. It would remain contingent that just this actual world was produced. God him-or-herself was bound to exist, but not I myself or you yourself, or our world. Only God and some creatures or other were bound to be. In contrast, the necessity of God is not for some god or other but for God as God. There need be no such necessity for any definite other being. Theism preserves the contrast between existential contingency and necessity.

God is 'unborn and undying' (an old Buddhist phrase with what reads like a theistic meaning), creatures are born and (as many Jews, some Christians, as well as at least many Buddhists believe) they will eventually die once and for all. The contrast between generated and ungenerated, mortal and immortal, is one of the grand contrasts given its full place by theism. This is less true when theists affirm personal immortality, thereby attributing one of the divine prerogatives to human beings. I think theists should accept death frankly and courageously. Nor do I find this a melancholy proposition. In the divine sense of the past our earthly careers are never to be blotted out, and in that sense we are indeed immortal. But so are all careers, however subhuman. However, only we can understand ourselves as imperishable contributions to the encompassing Life.

The wrong way of praising God loses the advantage of the theistic contrast by implying the unreality of the nondivine side. Consider, for instance, the contrast essential to human life between past particulars, already achieved by the "creative advance" (Whitehead) that is "reality itself" (Bergson), and future potentialities, not yet fully particularized. If God's ideal knowledge is supposed to span all time as a set of particulars, then the contrast between past and future, by which alone the universal-particular contrast can be understood, disappears. For God, as often defined, all is supposed to be wholly definite or particular. It follows that God has no purposes, by the very meaning of purpose. Here again theologians made things needlessly easy for atheists. Bradley and Bosanquet—and also, from a more purely monistic premise, many Indian philosophers—argued on such grounds against the idea of purpose as ultimate. But theism need not conceive ideal knowledge as abolishing the contrast between past and future, or actual and potential, or purpose and its realization. God, too, can be supposed to have an open future. Socinus in Italy and his followers in Poland (and perhaps those in Transylvania?) did this more than three centuries ago. God, they said, knows all things perfectly, the past and particular as that, the future, potential or nonparticular, as that. It is absurd to call "not knowing" future particulars ignorance when there are no such particulars to know. A judicious theism, and it alone, preserves all the basic contrasts.

Incidentally Wittgenstein did not say that belief in God was misuse of language. He merely said that he lacked faith. His position here is not altogether easy to grasp. And his admirers have split on the religious question. But which of them has shown much awareness of what has happened in metaphysics and philosophy of religion, beginning with Socinus and coming down to present day Process Theology? In this respect the impression I get of Wittgensteinians is of virtually complete ignorance.

CHAPTER THREE (C)

Extremes in Everyday life

PESSIMISM AND OPTIMISM

All animals face dangers and must act accordingly. If pessimism merely means admitting that genuine misfortunes are always possible and optimism means that misfortunes are only apparent since "Whatever is is right" and whatever happens is always the best possible in a best possible world, then this second extreme is false and pessimism as defined is true—though it is not an extreme. For false pessimism we must look to radical statements of the dark side of reality, such as that life is meaningless, or that in the long run nothing is right or good. Of course there are truly extreme situations in which, for instance, an individual has a disease well known to be fatal. If hope only means the expectation of continuing one's own earthly career for more than a few weeks or months at most, then the situation may indeed be hopeless. But there are other things to hope for.

One function of the idea of God is to give us a hope or goal that makes sense no matter how squarely we face the facts of our human situation. Some people try to find in social immortality, how future generations may benefit from our lives, a means of permanence for our achievements. But no matter how long our species persists, our permanent contribution to it, if any, would still leave much of our lives (whose value we are bound to feel every moment or we could not live) as "mere whiffs of insignificance," in the words of Whitehead. Only, so it seems to some of us, if we generalize social immortality to include God as universal Other, universal Friend, benefiting from *all* achievement of values by virtue of an allembracing sympathetic participation in creaturely experiences, losing no nuance of beauty or other intrinsically good awareness—only by this belief do we understand how the long future can "give our fleeting days abiding significance,' in the simple and sublime Jewish formula.

Although in living we must have caution as well as courage, avoiding the vicious extremes of life-denying hopelessness and reckless or stupid underestimation of dangers, there is no intermediate attitude that can be defined as uniquely right. Also, life would be dull if we were all equally moderate about everything. Pessimists sometimes make life more enjoyable for others. For instance, consider the one (he was the great scientist Sewall Wright, not the mythical "Murphy") who stated as a law of nature, "If anything can go wrong, it will." A dear late friend of mine (who was also a scientist of distinction) gave his own version of gloomy wit: "The two strongest forces in the universe are the condensation of things you don't want and the evaporation of things you do want." Note how environmental pollution can be included under the condensation and extinction of species, or reduction of their populations under the evaporation. My friend was an extremely knowledgeable ornithologist. Alas, however, this wittily pessimistic person came in time to see his own future in a seriously and unwittily gloomy fashion that, for all we can ever know, by the "depression" (as his ailment was in part medically diagnosed) may have shortened his life by decades. In contrast, Sewall Wright is still alive and able to walk vigorously in his nineties. Life is in principle hope, not fear.

QUANTITY, QUALITY, AND EQUALITARIANISM

Whales are vastly larger than human beings, their brains are in good proportion to their bodies; yet most people seem confident that whales are not of comparable worth to ourselves. (Some say that the question is not closed.) A child is smaller than an adult, an infant than a child. An infant's brain cells, we now know, are not fully formed—comparable, someone has said, to those of a pig rather than to those of an adult human being or even a child, properly so-called. Besides, in behavior an infant is not a "rational animal" in the sense that makes human beings superior to the other animals. By every test of quantity and quality a fetus is inferior to a child learning to speak, much more so to a normal adult. Yet many people are convinced, so they say, that the death of a fetus is a catastrophe comparable to the death of a child or adult. By what reasoning? "The fetus is alive and human, therefore..." What logicians call the "fallacy of ambiguity" could hardly be more unmistakable. That the fetus is a living but extremely immature specimen of no other species than that of its parents does not prove that it has all the value of its parents or even of a normal child. That is the very question at issue and is not to be settled by taxonomical classifications.

Let us now consider the doctrine of political equalitarianism. Jefferson said "born equal"; he did not say that an infant is equal to an adult, but that one infant is equal to another. It is also not hard to show that he had further qualifications in mind. He wrote about "natural aristocrats." In the context of his Declaration, the point was that people born in England were not thereby shown superior to people born in the colonies. He was, at least primarily, comparing groups, not individuals. He should have said further that skin color or African ancestry were not proofs of innate inferiority, and that sex was likewise no such proof. These steps have since been taken. But the matter is still insufficiently clarified.

What, if anything, is it that makes the human species of superior value to others on this planet? I think the answer is not hopelessly obscure. It is the capacity to think in the powerful way that only language, in an extended sense, makes possible for an animal. This extended sense is well called *the symbolic power*. Maps, graphs, mathematical and musical notations, arrows indicating directions, red indicating stop or danger, various gestures, are all included. These are what set us apart, so far as we are set apart, from the other creatures. We now know that Chimpanzees have this power in some degree—a far higher degree than any known human infant, yet, I think, not comparable to that of a bright child of five, or perhaps even of three years of age. But, to repeat, well above that of any known infant or fetus.

Why then the insistence that a fetus has an equal claim to be protected from the deliberate ending of its career with that of adults, or even of children learning to talk—which apes cannot do. The fetus, you perhaps say, can grow into an adult. Potentiality, then, is equal to actuality? This principle is hardly one according to which, in other applications, it would be possible to live. It potentialities are as good as actualities, why bother to strive to actualize theme? The goal has already been reached.

There is a secret source of the entire controversy. It is none other than *Noah Webster's Dictionary* in the unabridged edition. The word "person" is there defined in two ways, one of which appears to justify the extreme anti-abortion position and the other the (not necessarily extreme) pro-choice position. The one definition of person is "a human being", the other is, a being "able to reason and distinguish right from wrong." What a drastic difference there is between these two definitions, the one throwing no light on questions of human value, the other pointing to what is indeed an important difference between us and the other animals! Anyone in his senses can see and hear that women are linguistically like men, and that skin color or remote ancestry have no clear relation to the degree of symbolic power. Fetuses, however, are not at all linguistically like either men or women, but are like subhuman animals—which in a clear sense they are.

One of the marks of human superiority is the following. As we go down the scale of creatures, we find individual differences within a species diminishing until with species of atoms or molecules they seem to disappear altogether. *Individuation has degrees, and the higher the species the greater the individual differences.* This distinguishes us from all other creatures. It is not merely our lack of microscopic eyes that prevents us from finding differences comparable to those between Shakespeare and you or me in two ants of the same or not the same species. It is simply obvious that there can be no such difference in ants. When people talk of "personality" in dogs or horses they are greatly exaggerating a real fact. Of course, compared to ants or fishes of the same species, two dogs or horses are highly individual; but compared to two human adults or even children the reverse is the case. I conclude: although the difference in average inborn capacity among *groups* of persons sorted according to skin color or sex may, for all we now know, be small, perhaps negligible, the differences among individuals in each such group are large and for most purposes far from negligible. There is no easy way to measure the innate differences, since unequal opportunities and differences in the choices every individual is making every second of its waking life are bound to largely hide any innate differences. Nor can science predict them from knowledge of the parents. The mixing of genes from two parents is a gamble with virtually countless dice.

An ideal society is a friendly society; the ideal of friendship is equality. Hence there is a valid ideal in the equalitarian doctrine. But adequate individual freedom is also an ideal, and only severe controls could prevent some able or ambitious individuals from taking advantage of others' weaknesses to reduce them to subordinate positions. And whoever exercised the controls would not be merely equal to those controlled. The parent-child relation shows the dilemma. A parent can be friendly and should be; but it has to be assumed that the small child or infant is not simply another person; indeed the infant is only by courtesy called a person at all. Only the vaguer of the two definitions of the word applies to it.

Plato said, "perhaps no two things in nature are exactly equal." He meant, "in any respect." Equality is a limiting zero case of "greater or better than." It is the extreme exception, not the rule. I cannot but feel that many lazy or otherwise unmeritorious people in our democracy might be less lazy and more meritorious if they allowed themsleves to suppose that, as they are, they are not equal to some of the rest of us. Television flatters mediocrity of many kinds. I think there are persons superior to me and others less than my equal. But economic or social class is not the measure, nor is sex or race. Maturity does, however, have something to do with value. One of my favorite recollections is of meeting a member of another department (government) on campus one day and having him stop and remark to me, "Yes, there is an age gap, and *how I like my side of it!*"

Relations of quantity and quality are subject to extreme views other than those considered so far. Are two people twice as important as one person? If quality is equal, perhaps so. But if the number of persons in an area becomes indefinitely great, what happens to the quality of life? When deaths were largely determined by diseases and ailments not scientifically understood, and there was no effective technology for combatting them, it was necessary for women to have on the average many offspring so that enough would survive to reproductive age to maintain or gradually enlarge the population in a nature not yet badly polluted by the human species, then living simply and without the luxurious comforts made possible by applied science and stored energy. As death rates fall, energy is used up, and pollution becomes a serious threat, the question of population size acquires a different meaning. The admonition to the ancient Jews that they should "multiply" their kind is not now necessarily the relevant one.

The maxim of our culture often seems to be, if a little is good, more is better and still more better still. It is a false maxim. Are bigger cities better and the biggest best of all? Is Mexico City, the colossus, the ideal? Is New York? Chicago?

I am offended by boasts one encounters in restaurants about the large steaks, the "generous" portions of various foods served for similarly large prices. The fact is that with my size and mode of life, I have no use for these generous portions. At least a third of the population, especially women, are, I think, in something like my position. Restaurants seem determined to take into account chiefly the needs of large men, to the neglect of most of the rest of us. Result, one overeats, wastes food, or undergoes the embarrassment or inconvenience of asking for a "doggie bag," though one may have no dog or other pet. Some cafeterias are now beginning to go part way toward a reasonable compromise. Some dishes are offered—at long last—in two sizes! Chinese restaurants have always been better, since in groups each individual helps him or herself out of group dishes. I take this as one sign of the fact that the Chinese have been civilized for thousands of years. We are still serving meals suitable for our pioneer forefathers, who had to be physically active all day to keep from freezing or starving. How much food one needs depends, so far as seems to be known, primarily on one's size (apart from excess fat) and amount of physical exertion. Mental exertion takes far less energy, fortunately for those of us whose living is chiefly made by thinking. The difference is definite and has been carefully measured.

Another bad extreme is the way furniture is made. It is made in numerous styles but in essentially one size, that which fits large men and not some men and most women. I once complained to this effect to a woman sales person in a store. "Oh," she said, "furniture is not made for women!"

Of course there can be extremes of feminism. The division of labor between individuals cannot be wholly uninfluenced by the fact that only about half of the adult population, at most, is capable of producing offspring and partly nourishing them (in the best possible way) in or by their own bodies. However, the factor is far less important now that a much higher percentage of infants reach reproductive age, women live much longer, environmental pollution is a menace, and still other changes make the old patriarchal ideal less and less relevant. It still has *some* relevance. And all marked social changes cause trouble to some; we can neither simply forget our human collective past nor merely repeat old ways. We have to use partly old ideas and ideals to meet new conditions. I agree with the sociobiologist E. O. Wilson that, whether we simply drift along with the old patterns, *or* try energetically to bring about rapid changes, *or* adopt a more moderate attitude, for any one of these three procedures there will be a social cost.[C1]

Wilson leaves the issue a little too open for my taste. The cost may not be equal in the three cases. Our juvenile crime rate suggests we are not doing very well with the problem at present. I incline to the view that male chauvinism in most of its aspects is dangerously obsolete. Male ideals seem less and less able to protect us from catastrophe. The history of war is a startling affair, and it took a woman, Simone Weil, to put this aspect of human history as vividly as it needed to be put. Now with atomic bombs the potential enemies of all of us, men, women, children, the fetuses, we face an apparently hopeless dilemma: do without war altogether, a seeming impossibility, or run a very high risk of losing everything for which a war could rationally be fought. Before this dilemma we are in deep trouble. A new humility might become us. We belong to a species that gives signs of having lost its way.

We may despair—but my pious mother regarded despair as a sin, and I agree with her about that. Courage is still a great and needed virtue. But old-fashioned nationalistic patriotism seems inadequate to solve it? What then? "Love your neighbor" seems now to mean, your planetary fellow creatures—the human, but not wholly forgetting the nonhuman ones. Perhaps we even need to love the God of *all* creatures, not only those in our church, religion, clan, nation— or our species.

Economic Inequality

Although countries that have adopted socialist or communist forms of political economy do not so far furnish much evidence of the benefits of their departures from free enterprise, either for their own people or for the peace of the world, rather the contrary; still the present state of the capitalist countries is not a basis for much satisfaction in thoughtful observers. The dilemma, either nasty inflation or if possible nastier suffering by masses of unemployed ("stagflation") seems to call for some radical improvement in our economic system. An economist, Martin L. Weitzman, proposes what he calls a share economy, in which the present wage system is to be superseded, either wholly or in part, by a system of payment in which workers are asked to "receive a substantial part of their pay as a negotiated share of company profits or revenues (per employee). For bearing this risk, which is entirely voluntary, even though is is in the national interest, they will be rewarded by significantly lower tax rates."[C2]

The author makes what seems a reasonable case for this idea. As he says, Japan has gone at least partway in this direction with its bonuses to workers when things are going well. When we were in Japan some years ago, my wife, hearing about the bonus system, gave the admirable woman who helped us with cleaning and cooking a bonus after a time. This woman actually shed tears when we left Japan and said that in any future trip to her city we could count on her. The promise was kept.

To the objection that workers might not wish to take a share of the risks of business the author replies, The risk of total unemployment is what they bear now; why is that better than a lowering of income in recessions? Surely the answer is worth considering. What we have now is an ugly gamble. And excessive unemployment. The more I think about it the more I feel that the word 'share' is deeply right. We all share the planet together; religions tell us we are all brothers and sisters; we all do share risks; but we pretend that someone else is to have the risks and we will have the security. It is a seomewhat dishonest or cowardly affair. The present wage system is a humiliating one at best. The worker is treated as too stupid to see that the welfare of the company is his concern as well as his employers; all he can take into account is the size of his wage or other immediate benefits. Is he really that stupid? Should he gain nothing from the collective success and lose nothing (short of being unemployed) from collective failure?

Passing laws or resolutions against unemployment has not produced its intended result or anything like it. Why not reconsider the wage system as a substantial part of the reason for this failure? It is surely true that our lack of competitiveness internationally in a number of industries is related to the inflexibility of wage costs. What could the remedy be if not giving workers an agreed-upon share in both risks and chances of gain? There may be many complications hard for a noneconomist to see, but how can there not be some truth, in Weitzman's argument? We do share our planet, our country's good or bad fortunes and the well-working or ill-working of the institutions to which we belong.

The share economy idea has some similarity to Mortimer Adler's admirable ideal of ''universal capitalism,'' the only good alternative he can see to our present ''mixed economy.'' There is manifestly an ugly gap in this country and many countries between those with subhuman status and near zero participation in wealth and power and those living with vast extravagances and wielding immense power. There must be better ways.

Behavioral Leftovers as Extremes

Life refrigerated, cooked but not entirely eaten, foods, human patterns of behavior are partly left-overs, remainders of modes of action developed in the forgotten human past. The young see their elders doing certain things, so they do them. (Those with a vested interest in their doing the things help them with advertising incitements. Think of the tobacco industry, or the soft- or hard-drink industry. The soft drink purveyors can, I suppose, claim to be recommending a lesser evil.) Many things are done because they have ''always'' been done. The catch, however, is, not only have they not *always* been done—but there may have been a reason for their being done in the first place, and for centuries, that is no longer valid.

Why does nearly everyone drink tea or coffee? They are not nutrients; they do nothing to save us from starvation. They, especially coffee, are not cheap. They are potentially, often actually, harmful if one is susceptible to stomach ulcers—to mention only one possibility. Several other dangers are now known. Caffeine is, in quantity, a poison. In fifty cups of coffee (more of tea or chocolate) there is said to be a lethal dose of the stuff. Any good effects attributed to coffee or tea are largely illusory. One research found that coffee (whether one or two cups, I forget) reduces the blood flow to the brain by 25%. Is that ''stimulation?'' True, the heart beats faster, but when there is no need for it to do so. My father called tea a "true stimulant." He meant, compared to alcohol; but is tea really a stimulant? Why was such an addiction—what elso is it?—to these drinks formed by our ancestors?

My theory is that there are several historical reasons for the present status of these substances. Our species, being the only one that deliberately uses fire to prepare food, was bound to stumble upon the possibility of drinking hot liquids. Mild heat is an agreeable sensation, whether in the mouth or elsewhere. This is especially true in cold weather and in poorly heated houses. In England and Australia much warming of bodies is, or at least used to be, done from within. Moreover, boiling liquids eliminates harmful bacteria and other organisms whose effects were known long before they were. Hence drinking tea or coffee was safer than drinking unboiled liquids other than fruit juices or good spring water. As soon as people crowded into cities, this meant that they were considerably safer in avoiding unboiled drinks. Plain boiled water is at best rather tasteless, compared to fruit juices, which (unless alcoholic) were until recently largely confined to small parts of the year. So three reasons favored the flourishing of the habit in question: its superior safety (which would not need to be a conscious motive to have effects in the long run), its warming influence, and its non-insipidity. As soon as people realized the possibility of adding sugar, milk, or honey (which throughout history was known as a possibility) there was an additional favorable factor. Those not liking unrelieved bitterness, a rather sophisticated and somewhat unnatural taste, had an alternative. Of all these reasons at least two no longer have their original validity. City water has become fairly safe, and fruit juices are now obtainable all year round. They nourish excellently, are tasty, have vitamins. For the value they give they are not expensive, compared to coffee with its nonvalues.

I submit: the coffee-tea habit is a dubious leftover. It wastes human labor and non-rich people's incomes. Incidentally, for environmentalists and nature lovers, cofee plantations are aesthetically dull substitutes for lovely tropical rain or cloud forests in which (in Mexico at least) one of the most musical of all bird songsters (the Slate-Colored Solitaire, *Myadestes unicolor*) is found. Its future is doubtful as things are now, partly because it is caged for its wonderful song. I sympathize with countries of which coffee or tea are almost one-crop exports; but I suggest that they consider carefully whether they must be so limited to this one crop.

Is there not something wrong with the idea of "coffee breaks?" Why not fruit juice breaks? I deeply admired the Mormons on their university campus at Provo where, I found, there were no alcoholic beverages, no tea or coffee, but abundance of delicious fruit juices. How I enjoyed the latter! This is not the only respect in which I admire the Mormons; but it is one such respect. Of course there was no smoking. Think of all the preachers in other generations and other religions that either did not criticize smoking, or did so for much less than the strongest reasons even then obvious. These were: that it was a waste, with human labor and resources expended for no solid return; it was probably harmful, considering how unnatural a taste it is (no other vertebrate animal that I know of consumes tobacco in any form). And now the harm is known. Protestations to the contrary by vested interests are, to indulge in understatement, less than impressive. If any culturally inherited mode of behavior is a sign of human weakness and folly, is this not an outstanding instance?

There is, however, a complication. Tobacco is a mindchanging drug. It gives a mild sense of euphoria. In this it has some similarity to opium and its derivatives, also alcohol. Had the very serious dangers of the habit not been found, the case would have been much like that against tea or coffee. But they have been found. And there has always been another objection to smoking: it sets many fires and in that way causes many deaths and much destruction. An admired preacher and good friend of ours burned himself to death that way. The wife of a capable academic administrator I knew did the same. Before I stopped smoking I damaged a piece of furniture doing it. It has always been a dubious habit, more and more so as pollution problems multiply.

AESTHETIC MODERATION AS GOOD TASTE

Salt, except in small quantities, is a poison. If you doubt it, ask yourself why castaways in rowboats cannot drink sea water to avoid dying of thirst. Much American food is excessively salty. Even where this does no noticeable damage it is, I argue, bad taste. The reason is straightforward: no one, so far as I know, wants to drink even mildly salty plain water; some other taste is required to make a drink agreeable. From this I conclude that it is not the salt by itself that is enjoyed but the combination of saltiness and some other taste. Indeed it is a crude aesthetic enjoyment that derives from a single sensory quality. Simply putting sugar into water is no great aesthetic achievement; it is the combination of sweet and bitter plus some other sensory qualities that makes the charm of chocolate candy or liquid chocolate. If, however, the salt or sugar are excessive, then the other taste or set of tastes is scarcely appreciable and tends to lose its value. The right degree of bittersweet is alone good taste. Just where the optimum lies may be a partly individual matter; what is a general principle, however, is that the optimum here cannot be the maximum. The richness of life consists in a range of qualities each counting for something in itself. Sweetness is basically good; but the full beauty of experience lies in contrasts between various forms of goodness. There is much besides sweetness, mere agreeableness, in a Greek or Shakespearian tragedy; and they are valued partly for this reason. We enjoy the sublime, the ridiculous, and various other forms of aesthetic value as well as sheer beauty.

Although the various natural sugars are nonpoisonous, excessive use of them can have bad effects either by giving us quick energy and a false sense of being in fine shape while we neglect the proteins, vitamins, minerals, and fibers necessary for remaining in that shape, or by increasing an otherwise adequate intake of calories to the danger point that guarantees undue accumulations of fat.

If pepper is not a poison—and I wonder if it is entirely harmless to the digestive tracts of any of us—it is, in excessive use, bad taste for the reason already set forth. It nullifies the other taste qualities involved, reduces the enjoyment to a one-dimensional affair. And when people assume that everybody else will share their tendency to an extreme in this matter, I find it difficult to understand their obtuseness. If there is any way in which individuality should be allowed to express itself it seems that it should be to avoid having one's gustatory experience almost limited to a feeling of burning in the linings of the mouth or tongue. Or do some people have fantastically tough linings? I really would like to know, because I am genuinely baffled to understand acquaintances who have clearly wished certain others well and yet have offered them as a gift—even when one was an invalid—highly peppered food.

I remind the reader of my theory about the way leftovers from the past may partly explain unsuitable behaviors in the present. Before modern refrigeration, salt, pepper, contamination with smoke, extreme desiccation, were used to preserve foods. Made unappetizing to, or inedible for, bacteria and the like, they were yet tolerable to human taste. Then people got to liking them. Now with refrigeration, should we not rethink the matter? One need which the practice once met can now be met otherwise and, for all anyone has shown, more agreeably for most of us. Similarly, the large meals, often rich in fat as well, now served as standard in restaurants would have been right enough in a pioneer home when far more energy than now was required to withstand the cold and sustain the physically energetic life that nearly all then lived. Of course, if some are fanatic joggers, probably in excess of health requirements, they may need the meals in question.

I will probably be thought facetious if I mention another objection to tea and coffee: they add to household labor. The leaves or grounds must be disposed of, and the cups washed. For me this is not quite a negligible objection. Household tasks are a significant part of marital problems. *Either* women do it all (and in half the cases perhaps also go out to make a needed part of the family income, or even all of it in many cases) or husbands share the work. The more men do so, I think, the more they will come to wish that this work be kept down somewhat from the old days when nearly every man had a household semislave or two to do it. After-dinner coffee is one more nuisance for kitchen help—a voluntary role of mine during most of my fifty-eight years of marriage. It is time we learned to examine our behavioral leftovers for their appropriateness or lack of it to *our* situations *today*.

THE ILLEGAL DRUG PROBLEM

Applied chemistry has produced a proliferation of drugs that seems to have nearly overwhelmed our society, causing a great deal of folly and many tragic deaths. There are drugs prescribed by doctors, some of them less to cure ailments than to make people feel better with the ailments they have. If they live badly and in consequence sleep poorly, let them take sleeping pills. If they eat too little fibrous foods let them take a laxative. People have used alcohol since pre-scientific days to help them forget their troubles. They have used tobacco for a similar reason. But now there are many other mind-changing substances. Making most of these illegal is now being tried on a great scale. The drugs remain readily obtainable rather as alcohol did when it was illegalized. We keep inventing more and more utterly unusable weapons (because their use would threaten everything they could rationally be used for) but we cannot, or at least do not, prevent imports of illegal drugs in huge quantities.

He is wise indeed who knows how we are to save the country from this pervasive evil that has begun to reach quite young children. One doctor involved in the struggle seems to me to talk sense when he says that the greatest harm is still being done by the legal drugs. The two greatest outright killers are still tobacco and alcohol. Everyone who smokes is not only treating his or her own health prospects with contempt, but is setting a bad example for the young to follow. If smoking, proven so deleterious, is still flaunted as a thing to do in public as well as in private, what conclusion are the young to draw about drug-use generally? The same goes for any but genuinely moderate and cautious use, or avoidance, of alcohol. I find disgusting the way actors and actresses are still expected to smoke in their performances as though there were nothing wrong or silly in the behavior. When and where do the young see their elders acting with sense and restraint? Years ago, when youngsters were saying, "marijuana is no worse than alcohol," I kept wondering when they would realize that the implication was, marijuana is a very dangerous substance, which might easily destroy them and those dependent on them. The distinction between legal and illegal is a serious one enough; but it should not be allowed to blur the distinction between useful (or harmless) and deleterious or dangerous practices. That alcohol is horribly dangerous for many is a proven fact.

The Amerindians smoked before anyone else did, but how much? It was a ceremonial practice, as I understand it. It was not cigarette smoking, the worst kind. Did anyone make a living by providing it?

I sympathize with the drug administration, the FDA, but I still wonder why they allowed drugs that are dangerous if used with alcohol to be sold without notice of this danger on the bottle. One of the most miserable evenings I ever spent was after taking a single Anacin pill and drinking (*half a small* glass of) beer, both extremely unusual actions for me. I did not dare move for an hour, my feeling of abnormal misery was such; finally I slept an hour or so and awoke feeling miserable still. I was a fool, but why was it allowable to have no warning on the bottle? I found the danger was known to some of my friends. Did the experts in the bureaucracy not know of it also? In any case my long-time suspicion of the sellers of mind-changing drugs was confirmed by the experience. I cannot help hoping that the recent deliberate introduction of poisons into drugs will cause people to try to avoid pain less by drugs and more by following good health rules about diet, exercise, and old-fashioned sensible living (not working too hard, or living too lazily either; eating less fat and sugar and only a reasonable amount of protein, but ample amounts of fiber, fruit, vegetables; finding ways to control one's temper and avoid excessively negative attitudes. We are in danger of underestimating the "wisdom of the body" and vastly overestimating the wisdom or altruism of commercial chemists offering us their substitutes for right ways to enable our bodies to function. Insomnia is much less dangerous or harmful than sleeping pills can easily be. I know what insomnia is like well enough, and I know that moderate exercise, eating sometimes in the night, and avoiding too stimulating work late in the day do more than I see reason to think pills could do and with far less danger than the pills. I've never tried the pills, but I see no reason to reject the judgment of some psychiatrists that the pills cause insomnia more than counteract it. If you want to live well, look more than twice at chemists offering you remedies; get a good doctor and trust him, but take care about advertisers who certainly want your money, whatever they may want about your health. If you want your children to be careful and courageous about drugs and peer pressures, set them an example yourself in both respects. Give nature a chance, limit your resort to medicines supposed to make sound lifestyles unnecessary. Look for enduring creative long-term interests as modes of satisfaction, not some mere feeling of being "high" that produces no results that relate you to others in ways mutually beneficial and that may make you dependent on some substance, to get which you may do terrible things to others and ruin your future.

Long ago I came to the decision that I would not be dependent on any substance that is needless for health. I gave up coffee and tea, and found I was in no way worse off. I gave up tobacco (I had never smoked heavily) and was better off. To become dependent on some needless substance is to put oneself into a prison. To avoid dietary deficiencies seems problem enough without burdening oneself with an artificial need for things the lack of which does no harm whatever to a reasonably living person. In all these renunciations I was certainly better off in having that much more money to spend for a good life for myself or a friend or relative, or some cause I believed in.

POLITICAL MODERATION

My intensive experience in philosophical—and also ornithological—
inquiry, including much exposure to the history of these subjects,
does not mean that I am necessarily wiser than most people in making
political judgments. For me these are the most difficult, baffling
puzzles of all. But I have been observing politicians (recently, thanks
to C-Span especially) and puzzling over them with some care for
close to seventy years. So I venture to add a few remarks.

A wise man has said, "power always corrupts, and absolute
power corrupts absolutely." Ours is a powerful country, and only
one other today is similarly powerful. Are we corrupted by this
power? President Carter was keenly aware of the danger and tried
hard to warn and guard against it. By bad luck as much as anything
he was defeated. His successor is proud of having made us "standing
tall." Many like him for this. Carter is a much more knowledgeable
man, at least in many important ways (and so is Gary Hart), but people
do not always like those who know much more than they do. They
feel at home with Reagan in a way they could not with Carter. We are
all influenced in politics by personal factors that do not always have
much to do with solving the primary practical problems facing the
country. For some of us Reagan is unappealing, but not so for many
others of us. (For me Mark White, Governor of Texas, is more likable
and intuitively convincing than Reagan can ever be.)

Let us return to the point that ours is a powerful country, militarily with only one rival, though economically no longer so preeminent
as we had long been. Think of the mighty British empire. Where is it
now? How far was the British predominance a blessing for the rest of
the world? Who can say. Have we benefitted the Philippines by our
impirealism there? we treated them very shabbily at the time we
took them over from the Spanish; about this there is no room for
argument, I believe, though probably most of our population is ig-
norant of what happened then. And how have the islands fared since
we gave them a sort of independence? How did our economic and not
wholly unmilitary domination influence Cuba and other Latin
American nations? How many of our citizens have ever *honestly* considered these matters even for a half hour or so. Does standing tall
mean never doing such things?

How do powerful, large countries tend to differ from others? I am not alone in the following views. A large country insulates its citizens from awareness of other countries, a powerful country makes them think they do not need to speak foreign languages. In small countries, to be anybody one must do better than most of us do with other languages, must be less provincial. I have had one grandparent who spoke with a foreign accent and have known some realtives of her family who were Swiss and some who were Dutch citizens. I know what polished, several-language-speaking gentry they were, and may still be. (Otherwise, my ancestry is entirely Anglo-Ameican.)

I think it is simply a fact that our country's size and power have definite and marked disadvantages and dangers. Part of the challenge is to do what we can to surmount the disadvantages and ward against the dangers. I hope we will soon have a president who will do this better than our present one.

The problem of democracy is the old Platonic one—not that Plato reached the best conclusion here; but he saw some real aspects of the problem. How can those wiser than most of the people persuade them to take advantage of this wisdom? How can they make themselves known to and liked by people many of whom are less broad in their sympathies, less stable in character, or less skillful in understanding masses of people and various kinds of countries.

Bearing in mind that the use of nuclear weapons bids fair to destroy any values they could be used to obtain or defend, and that we are no longer undisputed superiors in economic skills, how can our country not only cooperate with those countries sharing our political ideals but cooperate even with Russian leaders with whom we do share something important, that they and we want to survive, rather than be blown up in a world-wide swirl of poisonous dust, leaving hopelessly unsafe drinking water, hopelessly contaminated milk, who knows what else that is horrible?

This section, indeed much of this chapter, would if they ever saw it seem to some people Unamerican. "He has no pride in his country," they would say. Well, I do have pride in this country. For me, Washington, Jefferson, and Lincoln are classic cases of men of power largely uncorrupted by this power. Our founding fathers contributed more, and we, by continuing on the whole to honor them, have contributed more to the theory of political values than any other national group in the past twenty-one decades. Emerson was one of the noblest and least provincial great men of letters. Robert Frost was a superb poet. Our philosophers, from Edwards to Peirce, James, and the Anglo-American A. N. Whitehead compare very well with European philosophers of their times. In fairly recent political history our treatment of conquered Germany, Italy, and Japan after WW II was a model of how to make peace. General Clay in Germany, MacArthur in Japan, and my former colleague T. V. Smith of the University of Chicago in Italy all understood that fighting and losing a war is "punishment" enough for a people—something the Northern states did not (after the death of Lincoln) altogether understand. These are reasons enough for us to cherish our tradition. There are also reasons for the citizens of a large and powerful country to bear in mind the temptations this exposes them to.

There is something else we should bear in mind. The entire Western tradition has been powerful and geographically extended. Indeed its power has for centuries now until very recently covered the globe. Its most pervasive religious tradition, the Judeo-Christian, has been deeply ambiguous about the role of military power. The God of significant parts of the Old Testament is a God of war. Simone Weil was so shocked by this that she finally became a rather unorthodox sort of Christian. But the ambiguity runs through the history of Christianity. Jesus and Paul, members of a people who had lost their worldly power, are one thing, the church militant is another. There is the Inquisition. A "stain (to adapt a phrase of Peirce) on the human mind itself." There is the holocaust, which not a single powerful nation did anything to check before the war started. Indeed it has been shown by some historian that every nation around Germany, and the U.S.A., gave Hitler unnecessary aid in his rise toward world dominance.

There is still another flaw in the Western tradition, compared particularly to Buddhism, but also to Hinduism, Shinto, and Confucianism. This is the extreme individualism of Western metaphysics. The world consists of individuals, each changing through time yet also in some absolute sense identical at all times of its existence. The directly rational thing to do is to advance one's own welfare. Acting for the welfare of others is then rationalized only by appeal to enlightened self-interest. Self-identity is treated as a pluralized absolute, diversity of these identities also as absolute. Buddhism, paralleled by and perhaps influencing Whitehead, had a different metaphysics of individuality. I as an infant (or even I a second ago) and I now, are not absolutely identical; neither am I absolutely non-identical with you. The great apostle said it, taken literally, "ye are members one of another." Whitehead's doctrine is even clearer on the same point and with the same ethical relevance. Altruism is just as directly rational as egoism. Jesus, in "Love thy neighbor as thyself," again taken literally, is on the Buddhist side. The idea of the self as simply other than one's neighbor is an unenlightened idea and ought not to enter the discussion. What am I, supposing my parents and other relatives, Plato, Peirce, Bergson, Whitehead, Emerson, had not existed?

Hinduism in the Advaita Vedanta form gets similar results, less analytically and rationally in my opinion, by saying that the diversity of individuals is Maya, not quite real; there is indeed absolute identity but it is non-plural. Some Hindus are moderately pluralistic and can take the theistic form that I incline to attribute to Jesus, but not to the classical theists of the middle Ages and most of the Reformers.

In China, both pre-communist and communist, it is taken for granted that one's purposes directly take others into account. One respects oneself only as member of a family, and the local and national communities are the superfamilies. In a televised study of China today the importance of this is brought out. We Westerners have been nourished by a metaphysical half truth about individuality. The Leibnizian Monadology in one of its aspects is the unconscious caricature of this error.

The opportunity in metaphysics today is that everything has been tried by now, taking the globe into account. The weakness of the Chinese tradition is the absolutizing, not of the individual but of the community, Hence communism could take over. Pluralistic Hinduism and Christians or Jews who return to the best in their traditions can, within human limitations, combine the advantages of all the doctrines. Even the Chinese can do this if they return to Confucius in his idea of Heaven, as some scholars interpret it, as truly theistic. But Confucius was one-sidedly political, did not do justice to the private aspects of personal relations. Above all, he was an atrocious male chauvinist, and in this gave the Japanese a bad model from which they still suffer. Marxists by preaching equality of the sexes, much more in theory than in practice, gained advantages by this in China and Russia, and no doubt elsewhere.

OUR SQUANDERING OF ENERGY

Another subject about which we need new ideas is energy consumption. Because stored energy gushed out of the ground, or could be dug out of it, we thought we could exert any amount of power and keep on doing this in order to enjoy all sorts of luxuries, some of them frivolous in the extreme, some of them harmful, as is auto-racing in which lives are lost and a lot of oil expended. We have been overheating in winter, overcooling in summer, and not even, in nearly all cases, making everybody comfortable. Frequently, one suffers from chill in hot weather. And it becomes impossible to dress for outside temperatures without suffering indoors, and vice versa. So people give up the outdoors (except as traversed in cars) and suffer from lack of exercise. Then they try to avoid this trouble by jogging.

It is now clearly unpatriotic to waste energy. It makes us perilously dependent on a few foreign countries. Yet the waste goes on. One-story houses are wasteful: they waste several things: roofing, energy to heat and cool, and space—causing cities to spread out excessively into the surrounding country without bringing very much of the riches of nature within the reach of city dwellers. Nature lovers perhaps have overlooked this. In Europe if much of nature is still left it is partly because houses to live-in mostly spread upwards two to four or five stories, not outwards.

A further objection to one-story dwellings is that they give less exercise than climbing stairs provides. I am quite sure that many people have lived longer bacause they climbed stairs (as my parents did) a number of times daily. My father ran up stairs, three flights of them (there was a basement) most of his life. He also, for many years, walked up a steep hill to his house five days a week. He lived into his eighties in good health and only died then because, in a moment of absentmindedness, he gave himself a severe electric shock that, it seems reasonable to conclude, brought on the heart failure that killed him some weeks later. As energy again becomes, as it surely will, in short supply, as space becomes more and more cramped by what a naturalist friend calls our rat-like breeding (taking most countries into account), we will have to reconsider many things about our standard of living. We will have to pay more attention to the difference between what we must have for a good life and what we only carelessly imagine we must have. The hidden price for our luxuries will not always remain hidden. It includes toxic wastes, for instance, a massive problem indeed.

The low standard of living we think of as that of third-world countries has its good side. Each of the American middle class burns up far more unrenewable energy than each of those teeming millions elsewhere. Can the world be expected forever to put up with this sort of thing? It has become an obligaton to moderate one's demands upon human labor and resources. The Asiatic ideal of holiness, living simply and reducing demands on the ultimately always limited environment, is basically sound. Executives who command enormous salaries but ask wage-earners to accept lower wages I find unimpressive as models to admire or imitate. Perhaps they need to set better examples of moderation.

We need an ethics that takes our crowded, pollution-and-annihilation-threatened world realistically. It sickens me to encounter diatribes about the destruction of comparatively mindless fetuses in a world that insists on preparing itself for a kind of warfare that could destroy men, women, children, and fetuses by millions or billions. We have truly monstrous evils to worry about these days. They are all related to our underestimation of the value of moderation on all of the many dimensions of life. If killing of fetuses, sad to be sure, is so terrible, what about the slaughter of whales, in their actual behavior and brains incomparably superior to any fetus?

Is there nothing, perhaps you ask, that there cannot be too much of? Yes, wisdom and love, which in their highest forms are really the same. Both Christian and Jewish Scriptures, and some forms of Hinduism, perhaps by implication all the high religions, tell us to love God with all our hearts, minds, souls, and strengths and our neighbors as ourselves. If you cannot believe in God, then say, the cosmic whole. Strawson in this context says, the universe; Jaspers the Encompassing. It cannot be merely the human species, for that contradicts our love (to wholly lack which is inhuman) for the other animals and nature generally. I am afraid that the effort to transcend every form of theism and still fully meet human needs will not succeed, and I take it as a fact that it never has succeeded in the past of civilized societies.

I close with a quotation from a much admired leader of reformed Judaism, Rabbi Olan, whom I have been privileged to know.[C3]

Consider the life story of one modern man. . . . It is not
fiction. His approach to the goods of this world is to use no
more than is barely necessary. . . .In the winter he sets his
thermostat at 68, and in the summer at 78. To use more
energy is to deny it to those who have little or none. . . . He
is a sensitive human being who is very conscious of so many
people on earth who possess nothing and use almost nothing.
It will take a world population endowed with these qualities
to reverse the human rush toward self-destruction. The
possibility of so radical a regeneration of the human creature
is very dim. . . . In conditions not unlike our own, the
Hebrew prophets offered one hope—if men do justly, love
mercy, and walk humbly they may overcome. Is it too late?
This is what Hillel meant when he asked: "If not now,
when?"

CHAPTER FOUR (D)

The Aesthetic Meaning of Death

"Death is the mother of beauties."—Wallace Stevens

To understand death we must know what life is; for death is the absence or cessation of life. A writer for *Life* and *Time* spoke of a tropical rain forest as a scene of death because animals consume animals, and plants bring about the death of other plants. This is as though a doughnut were to be described as a hole in a fried article. A doughnut is the part of the article other than the hole. And a forest teems with life, not death.

It can also be said: to understand life we must know what death is. The hole in the doughnut does contribute to the shape of the doughnut. If death is genuinely the cessation of an individual's living, the termination of a single career, then that career has definite character, once it has reached its temporal end. But if, as some say, death is like sleep, from which we awaken in another realm or mode of existence to continue our individual careers, then those careers lose their definiteness if the new career is really endless. And if not, there must be a death beyond death. Reincarnation ideas spell this out. I cannot believe that either of these ways of depriving a career of its definiteness is correct. I believe in the final definiteness of a human career and propose to argue that this is as it should be.

What is life? It is most fundamentally *aesthetic creation*, the achievement of harmonious experiences. That the most fundamental

51

and universal values are aesthetic can be seen in a number of ways. Ethical values cannot be the universal ones; for infants and the lower animals cannot exhibit them. But infants and the lower animals can enjoy harmonious experiences. They also suffer from inharmonious ones, as when they are frightened or frustrated in doing what they have the impulse to do. Cognitive values can hardly be universal; for how much can an infant realize them? It is the artist who is concerned with universal values, not the scientist and not the moralist. The artist values experience as experience, not as mere means to knowledge or other ulterior end, such as the future welfare of self or others. In this respect our Anglo-Saxon-American culture has perhaps more to learn than any other.

Aesthetic value can be missed in several contrasting ways. They know little of beauty who think that ugliness is its opposite. Rather, as we saw in chapter I, beauty is a mean between two opposites, of which ugliness is close to one. The other is mere orderliness, unrelieved by any element of surprise or irregularity. In what (for a given subject) is mere chaos or disorder there is for that subject no aesthetic value; in mere regularity or monotony there is also none. As chaos is approached, we suffer confusion or frustration, and call the situation ugly. As mere order is approached, we suffer boredom, lose interest, and call the situation monotonous. At either extreme experience itself lapses. While waking life goes on, we are between the deadly extremes and achieve some aesthetic value. Even ugliness is more interesting than mere lifeless order.

The mean between the extremes can be achieved on different levels of intensity or complexity of experience. There are intense sufferings, intense enjoyments, and tepid sufferings and enjoyments. Intensity seems to depend partly at least on variety and contrast. The richer the contrasts that are integrated into an experience the greater the value. Here, too, beauty is a mean. For we use the term "pretty" for the less intense forms of harmony, those not drawing upon our full capacities to integrate wide contrasts. Also, where contrasts are very great and we feel our capacity to assimilate them transcended, we are more likely to use terms like "sublime" or "magnificent" than "beautiful." I seem to be the first philosopher to discover that beauty is a mean. Aristotle said this of virtue, not of beauty. Virtue itself, so far as it is a mean, contributes to the beauty of experience, both directly and in its effects upon self and others. Virtue that does not do so is dubious virtue.

Aesthetic wholes are definite and finite. They could not be definite and wholly infinite. Mere infinity is formless, as the ancient Greeks realized better than some modern theologians have done. If God were wholly formless, deity would lack beauty. Hence, "infinite" is a poor synonym for "divine."

Works of art are finite. We expect a novel to have a last chapter; a poem, a last verse; a symphony, a last note. But we rather oddly seem surprised that a life, too, has a last chapter, verse, or note. If life is at all analogous to a work of art, we can, in this analogy, find a clue to the meaning of death.D1

Death is the solution for the aesthetic problem set by the very nature of individual experience. To be an identical individual is to embody over and over again one's individual "identifying characteristics." On the human level these become what we call personality traits. They imply a considerable degree of repetitiveness in the person's experiences. One's identity is an aesthetic theme on which each new moment of life is a variation. Themes normally admit a finite, but not an infinite, number of significant variations. Beyond that, the variations become trivial. Observation of young animals, human or subhuman, discloses creatures for whom life is new and exciting. Old people, old dogs and cats, are less intense about life. This is not a merely physiological fact, it is also psychological. It is explicable by aesthetic laws. In youth—and Conrad's novel of this title expresses this—how new everything is; in age how old and all too familiar! Death is the appropriate solution of this problem. It means new individuals, new themes, as well as new variations on old themes.

The question about death so far considered is, 'Why mortality?" Why are creatures incapable of living forever? There is a further question: How and when should death occur? This question is more complicated. For there are many ways of dying and many times at which it may occur.

First, we should note that the precise manner and time of dying must be contingent if anything at all is contingent. For very slight causal differences can decide between life and death. Only in a world where all things were determined by absolute power to the last item could the manner of death be predestined. I consider this idea of a single all-determining power to be as devoid of philosophical as it is of scientific merit. Theology should have nothing to do with it. For it means that the only real freedom is divine, that even man is like a puppet in the hands of God. If the puppet praises God, this is merely God praising God. If the puppet disobeys God, this is God disobeying God. We may well leave such nonsense to those of our ancestors who managed to come to terms with it.

The time and manner of death then are accidental. No divine purpose is illustrated in it. (For some this will be a hard saying. Superstition, or what some of us view as that, dies hard.) If, then, a life is a work of art, it is one peculiarly subject to chance interruptions and premature endings. It could not be otherwise, so fragile is a life in its hold on existence. In this sense all life is tragic and must be accepted as such. Even the divine life, as some of us conceive it, is influenced by this tragedy; for though that life cannot die it can share in our grief and vicariously feel our fears about death. Life is a perpetual gamble, one aim of which is, with luck, to arrive at a ripe old age, with one's individual capacities developed to their fullest and used in suitable ways. However, I submit, this aim is not the absolute aim, which is rather to make each moment contribute optimally to life in the future, one's own future so long as one survives, the future of others whom we may benefit, and above all and including all, the future of the divine life. This last, for the form of religion I find adequate, is the absolute aim; and even chance need not prevent our achieving it. In every moment, we can optimize our contribution to the divine glory. All other aims are subject to frustration. In this sense the service of God is perfect freedom, freedom from fear. It depends only on us, at least so long as we retain our sanity and self-control.

The reader may be wondering if what has just been said about God is consistent with the proposition that value requires definiteness and finitude, including the finitude of having a beginning and ending of a career. The divine career, if one can so speak, must be without beginning or ending. It also must not be confined to a portion of space. In these respects God is not finite simply as we are finite. The traditional use of "infinite" for deity was not wholly wrong. But the issue has been oversimplified. Our limitation, compared to God, is not sufficiently identified by the term finite. The point, more precisely put, is that we are mere fragments of reality, mere parts of the space-time whole. *Fragmentariness, not simple finitude,* is the mark of our being nondivine. God is unique in being nonfragmentary, in being the "encompassing" one, as Karl Jaspers puts it.

That God is nonfragmentary does not imply that the divine life is wholly infinite; for, though it has had no beginning and will have no end, at every point in the Creator-creaturely relations the creatures could have acted otherwise than they have, and God could have responded otherwise to their actions. This is only to say that neither God nor the creatures act merely mechanically. They keep making 'decisions', using this term in its broadest sense to imply that an agent could have done otherwise. Both philosophy and science have, for about a century now, been engaged in revising the classical idea of causality to make room for decision in this sense. Even a radioactive atom has (however unconsciously) to decide when to lose its radioactivity and change into an atom of lead. No known natural law will decide this for it, the law being merely statistical.

The idea of God responding freely to free creatures implies finitude; since "wholly infinite" must mean "actualizes all possibilities," whereas in each decision some one of the possibilities causally inherent in a situation is chosen and the others are rejected. To be free is to be able to do this, or that instead, but not both. Hence all actualization is finite, even divine actualization. God cannot have as actual all possible worlds. To identify deity with the sheerly infinite is to identify deity with pure possibility, devoid of actuality. It is the opposite of what Thomas Aquinas intended to mean by his "pure actuality." Yet the divine finitude is all-encompassing: it is not, as ours is, only a fragment of actuality.

Although absolute infinity is mere possibility, and actuality, even divine actuality, cannot be in every sense infinite, yet in a sense the divine actuality can be termed infinite. As the creative process is beginningless, there must be an infinity of already actualized responses to an infinite number of creatures; and since it is endless, it must perpetually add to this infinity. Another way to express this is to say that the divine personality is unique in forming a theme capable of an infinite number of *nontrivial* variations. It is no more surprising that God should differ from all others in this respect than that he-she (sex being here irrelevant) should be the sole being whose knowledge encompasses the universe with infallible accuracy.

I wish to say a word about an aspect of nature that troubles Schweitzer and many others, the way species prey on other species, bringing about their deaths. I think Schweitzer is sentimental here. All animals will die, whether as prey or not. And they should die, as we have seen. What does it matter to a nonhuman animal that it dies as prey of another animal, rather than by a stroke of lightning or a falling tree? I think it makes no essential difference to the animal. Rabbits do not have their lives poisoned by the thought of the "cruelty" or ruthlessness of nature. This is Schweitzer's problem, not that of animals in general. After perhaps a million or more seconds of enjoyment of life the prey perhaps suffers for a few seconds, or a little longer, no appreciable portion of its life's experience. Would universal old age be a better bringer of death? Old age tends to mean tepid experiences for the latter portion of life. The percentage of intense harmonious experiences in the world would be diminished by this hypothetical change. I have little confidence in our human ability to instruct God concerning world management.

Life in general is basically happy. This is clear from the following considerations. Animal happiness consists in the harmonious exercise of natural functions. The very existence of a healthy organism is a harmony of parts and activities. Sick animals are the most likely to die; but in general animals are not sick. They are usually able to do what they need or attempt to do and hence are not frustrated. Natural selection guarantees that this is the rule rather than the exception. As an amateur observer of animals for more than seventy years, I am firmly convinced that suffering is secondary and satisfaction primary in the lives of creatures.

Humanity is, in some ways, the grand exception to the foregoing optimistic picture. The reason is not far to seek. The other animals are born almost knowing how to live. The "wonders of instinct" are wonders indeed. But we are born knowing little about suitable designs for living. One has to learn a vast deal from adults and to rethink what one learns to make it fit one's own case. We live much more by thinking, and much less by feeling and largely preprogrammed impulse, than the other creatures. We have far more freedom. Not that the other creatures have no freedom. I believe that they all have some, but it is relatively trivial in scope. The basic outlines are determined by the past. Creativity is minimal. But each human being has to work out a design for living that is his or her own. Why should these designs not sometimes conflict and impede cooperation among individuals? What could guarantee that this will not occur? Yet interindividual cooperation is essential for human existence.

That there is tragedy in human existence is then less surprising than most theologians have made it appear to be. They have not believed in the reality of creative freedom as universal principle and have falsely absolutized the causal influence of the past, or of the First Cause, making it all-determining of each new present. Assuming creative freedom, each creature is more or less at the mercy of chance interactions between its own decisions and those of its neighbors, human or nonhuman. Even without malice this may cause considerable unhappiness. And what is to insure that it will always be without malice? Can there be a thinking, selfdesigning yet not divine creature infallibly superior to feelings of anger or hostility, feelings without which an individual can not easily maintain its way in life? Infallibility is a divine attribute. Could even God make an infallible creature, a divine nondivine being?

When Buddhists talk of the misery of unredeemed human or animal existence, and when Christians talk about original sin, they are trying to face the deep tragedy of life on the highly conscious level that is human existence, as well as the general tragedy of life of any kind. They attribute frustration, suffering, anxiety, hatred, fear, and other evils at least partly to selfcenteredness, or greed. Each animal is to itself the center of the universe; it sees the world with itself here and other creatures there. We are animals in this sense, but as Reinhold Niebuhr saw so well, our species is unique in that each of us knows that he or she is not really the center. The conflict between the way our senses and selfserving imaginings give us the world and the way our rational thought tells us it must really be is the essential religious struggle. The self is not the center around which things revolve; but we are tempted to pretend that it is. Christians have called this sin and Buddhists have called it ignorance. It is a partly guilty ignorance; for we are capable of knowing better.

The solution for this troublesome problem Buddhists call Nirvana; Jesus called it "peace." So, no doubt deliberately, did Whitehead. I am convinced that the best so far presented philosophical explication of this idea is Whitehead's. I have already hinted at this view. Our experiences, and those we can influence for better or for worse, are all contributions to the Consequent Nature of God, by which Whitehead means that they add to the beauty of the universe as enjoyed by God, who is the genuine Center of the universe. In the words of Berdyaev, to which there is a parallel in Tillich, our lives "enrich the divine life itself." God participates in our happiness, in all our experiences. For Whitehead this is the real meaning of "omniscience." Adequate knowledge of feeling can only be "feeling of feeling"; adequate knowledge of the experience of another can only be experience of that other's experience. In all social awareness there is an aspect of sympathy, and in perfect knowledge this aspect is uniquely complete. Thus our momentary experiences become everlasting possessions of deity.

In human life suffering may loom large partly because in it sickness does not lead nearly so quickly or inevitably to failure in the struggle to survive as it does with the other animals. Predators, whose victims are likely to be the very young or the very old or the sick, have become a minor factor in our lives compared to those of most animal species. Medicine has acquired great skill in prolonging the process of dying by disease. Of course, this has its good side. Human beings make long-range plans; and longevity is much more valuable to them than it could be to other terrestrial animals. And medicine can also to some extent mitigate the suffering associated with disease. I am not convinced, however, that we have yet learned very well what use to make of the powers of medical technology to prolong life. Since we all die, and merely being alive on a subhuman level puts us below the plateau of worth that elevates our species above the others, it is childishness or mere superstition that brings it about that a dying man, for example, is, at great expense, and with the employment of resources that probably could be used for more important aims, kept breathing some days or months longer than otherwise might occur. No rational person should wish to have this sort of thing done in his or her own case. I do not.

Does the mere fact of suffering yield a reason for wanting to die? Perhaps it does, if the suffering distracts the individual from accomplishing anything beyond merely enduring it, and there is no chance of recovery. It happens that the suffering that I can recall having had to bear has rarely been so intense or persistent as to seem very important. The nearest to an exception has been an occasional bad headache (before I learned to live so as not to have headaches). By comparison any toothache, ulcer, spastic colitis, leg cramp, or postoperative ache that I ever had was relatively minor or mild. So it may be that I lack sufficient experience with really grim suffering to easily judge its endurability.

One aspect of suffering that is implied by the Whiteheadian view already sketched is that our sufferings are not merely ours, nor are our friends the only ones who sympathetically participate in them with us. Whitehead's words, "God is the fellow-sufferer who understands" are not only sincerely meant, they do follow logically from his doctrine and illustrate his category of "feeling of feeling" upon which, according to him, all social knowledge and indeed all knowledge of concrete realities is based.

From such a view of suffering no easy answer to the question, "How far can life be desirable when persistently attended with suffering?" seems derivable. I assume that all experience has some value, because I do not see what could keep us alive except a kind of will to live. Actions speak louder than words. And continuing to live consciously is an active partly voluntary affair. (I am not speaking of life in a coma; for in that state it is only our cells that do the living.) And I assume that so long as we gain something by living (and if not, we stop consciously living) God gains something by sharing in our experiences. But this is not the whole story. There is pithy proverbial clue to the meaning of an individual life, "Is so and so worth his salt?" All life is competitive, it takes something from other lives, as well as contributes to other lives. These other lives are also of value to God. The question, "Do I contribute enough to make a net balance?" seems, to me at least, to make sense.

How can such questions be settled by the principle that the duration of life should be left to God? Medicine has interfered in a thousand ways to disturb the kind of natural balance of births and deaths that might plausibly be attributed to deity. For ages human beings have interfered in such matters, and now more than ever. How can a thinking animal not do so? But the question remains, "What are the judicious modes of interference?" By devoting costly and scarce devices to keep some persons alive after neither they nor anyone else has much reason to desire their continuance, we condemn others to die long before their useful possibilities are exhausted. Our reverence for life is remarkably, and not very reasonably, selective and spotty. I cannot believe that we have yet reached finality of thinking about the ethical and legal questions involved here.

Those who equate abortion or letting people whose genuinely personal life is over die with "murder" in the proper normal sense are darkening counsel. A fetus is only the probability of a person, if that means, with Webster's most adequate definition, a being characterized by consciousness, rationality, and a moral sense. Neither a fetus nor a person in a final coma gives any evidence of a moral sense. To that extent it is indeed "innocent."

A probability of something is not that something, especially when the probability can only be realized by one or more persons making substantial effort and sacrifice. A fetus is not like a seedling in a forest which, with luck and being let alone, will grow into a mature tree; on the contrary, a fetus can become rational and moral only if a lot of human effort is devoted to that end. The opponents of the moderate Supreme Court decision on this subject are not, I imagine, usually ready to undertake this effort, and some of it only the pregnant mother can undertake. The mother is a person. I will be more impressed with the moral superiority of extreme opponents of abortion when I note them turning their attention to discouraging unwanted pregnancy and the ignorance and carelessness that bring it about. Is it life on a properly human level they are concerned about, or is it just life that might eventually reach that level?

In my view, life is a gift;and no animal lives entirely without wanting to do so, with the one exception of a purely vegetative kind of existence in which the real agents are simply the many cellular parts of the animal rather than the animal as one. But a human being with self-respect should not want to enjoy a mere remnant of human existence at the expense of others who need the resources he or she is using. Whether or when life becomes such a mere remnant depends on many things. Some elderly people are a valuable inspiration by their courage and generosity in adversity. (But persons in a coma are not being generous.) These questions, which the progress of medicine and hygiene has made so important and will make still more so, are difficult indeed.

Heidegger has had much to say about mortality not being merely the end of the process of living, but a determinant of its meaning throughout. We should learn to assimilate this meaning consciously. But Heidegger seems to make too little of the point that Whitehead and the Buddhists take as central, which is that the value of life is in experience, and that each moment's experience is a new actuality displacing the one that came before it (save so far as memory retains the quality of that previous experience). As Santayana brilliantly put it, each moment "celebrates the obsequies of its predecessors." Death is merely the final phase of this perpetual loss of values once enjoyed. Death should teach us what, from a sufficiently subtle point of view, should be apparent without regard to death, that the meaning of life essentially transcends the individual ego and its future fortunes and refers to a good to which the present moment may be expected to contribute, a good more permanent than the individual, yes, even than the species.

Believers in God can conceive this permanent good as the divine life inheriting by its loving omniscience all creaturely experiences. Unbelievers will have to content themselves with a vaguer faith that somehow the universe will be better by our having lived and having been more or less happy and helpful to others.

It may be easier to have such a faith, either in the theistic or the vaguer form, if we remember that the most skeptical person faces a somewhat similar puzzle if he or she merely asks the question, "What will make it always true that our experiences, each with its special qualities of joy, suffering, and the rest, really occurred?" These experiences no one else, in many cases, knew about at the time, and we ourselves have already largely forgotten them. Think of the ten or twenty thousand years before Columbus came to this continent, during which the Indians lived, enjoyed, suffered, perceived thought, each individual differently from every other, in various parts of the Americas. These individual qualities of experience of centuries ago are not now to be found anywhere in the two continents. There are only arrowheads, piles of clam shells, remains of dwellings and (exceptionally) some bits of writing or visual art. Is it then no longer true that there were such experiences, each quite definite and unique to the individual and the moment? The permanence of truth about past events is the same problem logically as that of value-qualities not now humanly enjoyed. The theist has an obvious solution, and it is the same solution that he has for the question, "Why will it be important, if it will, that we have lived well rather than ill?" If, in a no longer surviving tribe, before Columbus a certain man was good to a certain wife, is it still good that he was so, or is it now of zero import? And for that matter, what makes it still true that this good life did occur?

There seems to be nothing in all our science to indicate an answer to these questions. Philosophy and/or religion must answer them if they are to be answered.

The divine inheritance of our experiences means that, though death is the termination of our careers, it is not their destruction. To write "the end" after the last sentence of a book is not to destroy the book. A book is destroyed only when it can no longer be read. But at least God will read the books of our lives forever after. Are they worth this everlasting attention? The idea of omniscience implies an affirmative answer. It implies that nothing is uninteresting to God.

However, being interesting is a minimum value. The absolute aim of life, the sole aim that is beyond criticism, is to make those books of life that we have a part in writiing as valuable as we can. Only the divine reading can put any books "where neither moth nor rust doth corrupt and thieves cannot break through nor steal." It alone can "give our fleeting moments abiding significance."

Some will say that the Whiteheadian doctrine of the "immortality of the past" in God is still not personal immortality. I reply that there is nothing impersonal about a career; for each is unique in all space and time. This is no doctrine of loss of individual distinctness. We are not to be absorbed or dissolved in an impersonal absolute, as our bodies may be scattered by worms, or by water or wind. All of value that we actually are and ever have been between birth and death will remain. And so the vivid experiences that make up our lives, "though they perish [for our feeble memories], yet live forevermore" (Whitehead). This is the Whiteheadian view of what it means to love God with all our being, to live for the service of God as inclusive of all lesser ideals.

To trust God is to be confident that if our lives have the finitude they seem to have, this is as it should be. Mortality is too basic to life to be an accident but must either—as I believe—inhere in the very meaning of "creature," or be a divine decision with which as such no creature that understands its creatureliness can quarrel. With Robert Frost, I think that "earth's the right place for [human] love/ I don't know where it's likely to go better." For love on earth, love of many persons and creatures, and love especially for one or two persons (wife, daughter), I for one am deeply grateful.

CHAPTER FIVE (E)

Bias in Philosophy

TWO VIEWS OF METAPHYSICS

An antimetaphysical writer, Morris Lazerowitz, has suggested four ways of viewing metaphysical propositions: as (1) empirical, or (2) a priori true or false, or (3) verbal, or (4) linguistic innovations.[E1] (I shall hereafter refer to pages of Professor Lazerowitz's book by numbers in brackets.) Only the last view is accepted. I wish to argue that metaphysical propositions may well be both a priori true or false and (to some extent) linguistic innovations. Lazerowitz also holds [67] that there are three layers in metaphysics, "an illusion of a theory about the world. . . , a non-verbal sentence which embodies an alteration of language. . . , and a belief. . . , which satisfies a wish and counters a fear in the substratum of our minds." I wish to amend this as follows: bad or unsuccessful metaphysics, metaphysics which fails of its highest aim, does involve illusions of the kinds in question, and these occur at least partly for the sorts of unconscious emotional reasons suggested. However, successful or true metaphysics expresses no illusion but a necessary or a priori truth, not in particular about "the world," but about reality as such, about any and all possibilities or conceivabilities for worlds or thinkable states of affairs. The belief in this necessary truth does not satisfy any particular wish, nor does it counter any particular fear, but rather it expresses common factors relevant to all possible wishes and all possible remedies for fear, against no matter what.

The critical question, of course, concerns the possibility of distinguishing, on any reasonable grounds, between bad and good metaphysics. The nature of the contrast is at least crudely indicated by such commonsense expressions as "one-sided," or "unbalanced," versus "well-balanced"; "exaggerated," versus "properly qualified"; "extreme," as against "the golden mean." More technically the truth is the "higher synthesis" or, as Hegel put it, "the unity of contraries." I distrust much of Hegel's execution of the program, but this phrase, while needing careful interpretation, is acceptable. Now it is remarkable how frequently Professor Lazerowitz, like many of his contemporaries, takes as examples of metaphysics such obviously one-sided doctrines as, "substance is completely unknowable" [145], "things are but appearances" (thus quite knowable indeed) [1,32FF., 199]; "nothing exists" [181f., 189ff.], "we cannot perceive negative facts" [193]; "everything changes" [27f., 42, 46, 58, 63], "nothing changes," or "time is unreal" [1, 10ff., 13, 19–22, 27, 29, 36ff., 46, 58–79. 163–180]. I believe he also mentions, but does not discuss, "all relations are internal" or "all are external." Of course these contrary extremes cancel out, the one side being as defensible or indefensible as the other. But for that very reason both are valuable since their common absurdity helps us to find the golden mean or higher synthesis. By what magic does our author miss this point? Does he have an unconscious wish to miss it, and thereby to miss the point of metaphysics itself?

Possibly Lazerowitz's idea is that the higher synthesis would be simply ordinary good sense, and in no way a contribution, or anything exciting. But I cannot agree. The synthesis would indeed be harmonious with sound common sense, but on a different level of conscious explicitness. Let us see this in a particular case. We are told that "nothing changes" cannot be meant to apply to phenomena, since the metaphysician knows as well as anyone that phenomena exhibit change in the plainest fashion. Nor, for a similar, though perhaps less obvious, reason, can "everything changes" be meant to apply to the experienced world of fact. All well and good: but take, "Everything changes (at least eventually) except. . .", where the proper characterization of whatever it is that is absolutely and necessarily immutable is supposed to be furnished. That *this* statement does not apply to phenomena is less manifest; indeed, I hold that in a sense it does apply to them.

If by "reality" or "the world" one means whatever happens to exist, *taken in its contingent aspects alone,* then our statement says nothing about the world. But the question is, What is true of *all* the kinds of things that might conceivably exist (better, all the kinds of events that might conceivably occur, or again, "all possible kinds of world"? For example, would there, in *any* world, be causes producing effects according to some sort of laws, some order, and if so, would this order in all cases be of the deterministic sort (excluding randomness entirely), or in all cases partly indeterministic; or finally, in some possible kinds of world deterministic, and in others not? Lazerowitz would perhaps hold that the very possibility of speaking of deterministic and indeterministic laws (statistical, approximative, probabilistic) implies that both are logically possible. It does imply that there are deterministic and indeterministic aspects of conceivable laws; but whether either aspect would or could altogether exclude the other in any conceivable state of affairs is another question. Every competent person who has tried to carry through the analysis of a deterministic law, even on Newtonion presuppositions, has been impressed by the difficulties of avoiding absurdity. Thus Reichenbach concludes a careful discussion by saying that, though determinism is logically compatible with classical physics," it is an "empty," "redundant" addition to it, "which can very well be dispensed with."[E2] The "compatibility" itself is empty, unless classical physics could be literally true of some conceivable world. With Bergson, Peirce, and others, I view that physics, taken literally, as incompatible with the meanings of 'process,' 'event,' or 'time.' But it is also highly doubtful if the notion of a completely lawless or random state of affairs has a consistent meaning. Hence the partly indeterministic, or "intelligible chance," conception of law may be the sole truly conceivable view, valid for any universe whatever. It is then a piece of good metaphysics.

Of course, the foregoing metaphysical statement about law communicates no "fact," if by that is meant something in nature that might conceivably not have been as it is. But it does not follow that nothing has been affirmed about "reality." The real is that to which true affirmations refer. Metaphysical affirmations seek to put into conscious conceptual form whatever is common to, or true of, all conceivable occurrences. Is this common element of all possibility a mere matter of words or meanings in human discourse? This type of anthropomorphism is not self-evidently correct. Is it only our thinking that makes things possible, even "logically possible"? I hold that there would be actualities and possibilities (both "real" and "logical") were there no human thought, and that these would have a universally common element which by definition would be the necessary. Metaphysics is the attempt to characterize this element. It is of course no "fact," for this word is best used only for that which *contingent* true assertions affirm. But if reality is the object of correct affirmations (that which measures their truth), then the necessary can also be real. It is neither a fact, nor something merely "behind," or additional, to all facts; but rather, someting *in* them all. Is it "supersensible"? It is an element or aspect of the sensible, but not as such sensible; for it is experienced only in universal union with the sensible, from which it can be distinguished only by operations of thought. Metaphysical statements are not descriptions of particular things, but without them no description of anything is complete or fully explicit.

Metaphysics without God outdoes Hamlet without Hamlet. Like so many, Lazerowitz thinks that a "transcendently perfect Being" (a phrase in which I find a dangerous ambiguity) can be affirmed to exist, if at all, only as something entirely factual or contingent [27f.]. This is a typical piece of bad metaphysics. The opposite extreme, also bad metaphysics, is that God can only be conceived as exclusively necessary, entirely without factual or contingent qualities, the "necessary being" and nothing else. The synthesis is that God is the subject of both factual and *a priori* or necessary existential propositions, according to a principle deducible from the meaning of "divine perfection." Anselm saw one side of this and neatly missed the other, and this is one reason for his failure to convince. It can, I think, be shown that what even the plain man means by "God," as "Creator of all," entails that such a being could not just happen to exist, or happen to fail to exist. Contingency-of-existence is part of the meaning of "creature," and is excluded by the meaning of "creator of all" or of "supremely perfect." Contingent existence entails imperfection. We all have "existential" awareness of this. To be *capable* of nonexistence is to be imperfect, even though existent. Which critic of Anselm even discusses this point?

"Divine perfection exists"—if "existence" is meant in the factual sense— is quite as absurd, according to Anselm (in his reply to

Gaunilo), as, "Divine perfection does not exist."[E3] Either we have here a necessary truth or a necessary falsehood (absurdity), but in no genuinely conceivable case a mere fact, positive or negative. Nevertheless, granting for the moment that the divine existence is necessary (we shall later see another reason why it cannot be contingent), there must also be factual truths about God; and that which in God "makes" them true can only be contingent. Thus, "God knows that elephants exist" cannot be necessary, since it entails "elephants exist," which is not necessary. Hence God's knowledge of the existence of elephants can only be something non-necessary, a contingent or factual qualification of the divine. Here theology (with some honorable exceptions) for nearly two thousand years stubbornly adhered to a contradiction. It refused to admit anything contingent in God, yet asserted his knowledge of the contingent world. Why this stubborn persistence in what seems the plainest contradiction? Here something like the author's psychological explanation may be at least part of the answer.

The seeming paradox of an individual whose existence (not whose entire reality) is knowable a priori can be mitigated by adding a point which is relatively new in metaphysics. "Existential statements are contingent"—logicians are almost agreed upon this doctrine. But, like so many others, the statement turns out to require further distinction, refinement, or qualification. The refinement I suggest is that existential statements on the lower logical levels, those mentioning definite particulars, or special qualities of particulars, are all contingent. However, existential statements not mentioning definite particulars or special qualities, are a priori. For instance, "there are particulars" affirms nothing definitely particular or special, as "there are secrets" divulges none. Again, as will be explained presently, by "God" is intended an individual whose existence exhibits complete tolerance toward all special or particular existential statements. I hold, therefore, that it is a category-mistake, a mistake as to logical level, to take the existential statement, "an ideally powerful and wise being exists" as the affirmation of a contingent truth or a contingent falsehood—in short a fact, actual or conceivable.

It may seem strange to say that, though God is an individual, the divine existence is not anything particular. However, we must distinguish between things or persons, and events—only the latter being necessarily, and in all cases, particular. One of the pieces of unfinished business in current logic is the casualness with which things and events are lumped together as the values for the existential operator. (The author does not, so far as I can find, face this topic in the book.) The logic of the theistic question can scarcely be discussed profitably unless one distinguishes systematically between the level of actual occurrences, including human experiences, and the level of enduring things or persons. The latter is a different level, logically and metaphysically. Only occurrences are fully concrete, only they fully illustrate the law of excluded middle as to predicates. They are the ultimate contingencies, and the contingency of (ordinary) individuals is a logical function of their contingency. In the case of deity, it is part of the meaning of individuality on that exalted level that *any* particular event or state of the universe would have as its correlate an appropriate particular state of the divine individual (as in some genuine sense creator and infallible knower of that universe); hence the contingency of everything particular, even a particular quality of God, does not mean the contingency of the divine existence or individuality. If our author were correct in saying that metaphysical problems are simple and not especially subtle, I could have made all this clear in a paragraph! But as I am about to explain, I do not think that he is correct in this contention.

The essays before us argue that the a priori view cannot enable us to understand the endless, seemingly incurable, disputes among metaphysicians. For, says the author, metaphysical demonstrations are neither more complex nor more subtle than those of mathematics [39]. He does not argue this point. He perhaps thinks his examples of metaphysical propositions show how simple and unsubtle they are. To some extent this is correct; for he has in general chosen relatively simple and sometimes extraordinarily crude examples. They are practically all examples of bad metaphysics, one-sided extremes of a sort which few major speculative philosophers during the last century and a half have wished to defend. True, Bradley took a position of this sort, but as William James said, he was a brilliant man spoiled by "perversity," by an emotional bias making careful examination of issues impossible. James was on the whole less one-sided . Some others were less unbalanced than James, Peirce being one. Another is too obvious to mention. But our author ignores what I take to be the main stream of recent metaphysics.

Is metaphysics as simple as mathematics? In the first place, I suspect that metaphysics includes pure mathematics, for it includes all that is entirely a priori, free of essential empirical elements. In the second place, the simplest aspects of mathematics (and derivatively the complex aspects) are capable of a degree of clarity that other a priori knowledge cannot attain; and it is just this possibility of clarity that (among other considerations) causes the mathematician to select the topics he does select as parts of his subject. The secret of mathematical clarity seems to be the Peirce-Wittgenstein principle of structure exhibited in symbolic form, or as Peirce put it, the "observation of diagrams," symbolic arrays operated upon according to rules. In this way, e.g., the addition of units to make two, three, and so on can be made as simple and obvious as any a priori conception could be, and as capable of clarity. But the discernment of what is invariant in all logically possible change; or of that which makes it possible for there to be permanent truths about events which, because of their remote pastness, seem now to be as nothing; or the discernment of the common element in all conceivable causal laws; or of what can intelligibly be meant by "God"—how can these be made simple and crudely obvious? In my opinion, the large majority of the greatest minds that have considered these topics have fallen into more or less confusion about nearly all of them. Lazerowitz urges that this confusion—as shown by the inability to agree—can be explained only by supposing that unconscious drives have been motivating the procedures [67-79]. I accept much that he says about this. But does it invalidate the view that metaphysics is the search for a priori truths which really obtain and might, to a greater or lesser extent, be known by human beings? I see no either-or here, but a both-and.

The one-sided errors which mark the failures of metaphysicians are indeed, in one sense, all too evidently successes, namely emotional ones. If what you fear is change, how comforting to deny its reality! Or, more subtly, make change itself (verbally) the one permanent thing, and in this way attain a sense of immunity to particular changes. Or perhaps, if fixity bores you, exult in the notion that even the hills are not everlasting. Or, if you dislike the irksome restraints of material limitations, deny the reality of physical things. Please note, however, that anything which can be said concerning the appeal to the unconscious of one-sided or bad metaphysics is quite compatible with the view that there *could* be a balanced or correct metaphysics. Indeed, the fact that metaphysical one-sidedness has emotional values strengthens considerably the case which Lazerowitz cavalierly rejects—the case for the view that a priori metaphysical truth is *neither* an illusion *nor* at all easy to find and keep in sight. It is not easy, partly for intellectual reasons of subtlety and complexity, to which our author does much injustice, and partly for the very reasons of emotional temptation which he so well elucidates. What inconsistency is there in thus combining these two points?

Furthermore, it is impossible to do justice to metaphysics unless one realizes that, as there is a distinction between contingent fact and necessary truth, so there is between ordinary first-level wishes or emotions—contingent demands or preferences which can be renounced for good and sufficient reasons, whether of non-possibility of fulfillment, or of prior claims—and whatever may be common to all possible wishes or demands, so that to renounce it would mean to deny life itself. (Even the suicide does not really do this; for his deliberate attack upon his own life is a positive act, whose value he in effect affirms.) Now my proposal is this: Sound metaphysics resists the temptation to bolster any *contingent* values by a priori pronouncements; but the effort to find a theoretical formulation for the noncontingent "demand" which is inherent in life as such is a legitimate endeavor, and not a yielding to temptation at all. For what it affirms is what everyone affirms, merely by living and acting; the only difference is as to the degrees and clarity with which one formulates the affirmation in concepts. The feeling that one does not want to die, or to change, or to admit the reality of death or of change, is a contingent demand, which *can* and *should* be renounced! But the insistence that neither death nor change can mean that the universe ultimately might in no way be enriched by one's having existed and thus that all one's efforts to serve a long-run good might be totally defeated—the validity of this insistence is not contingent, and is in effect accepted merely by living. Indeed its denial is nonsensical; for as Santayana notes—without full realization, I think, of what is involved—it must always remain true that one has lived as one has, more or less happily, and with more or less benefit to others; moreover, the notion that this permanence of truth carries no implications for the permanence of any other values arises, I should argue, from faulty analysis, or lack of analysis. Some sort of "immortality" is already accepted by those who admit that truth is indestructible and this may be the only immortality we need for any essential purpose of giving life a "meaning." But more may be involved in the immortality of truth than non-metaphysicians, and perhaps most metaphysicians, quite appreciate. "Truth" is but a word—what "makes" some statements true for all the future?

It is easy to say that life need not have any permanent value-result; but I am not aware by what mode of action it would be possible to show that this affirmation has more than verbal status. With Schweitzer, I take it as a verbal gesture, contradicted by itself and by any and all gestures taken as expressive of life. Life includes faith and trust in the future, beyond any time limit that can be set; not necessarily in a self-regarding future—I am not talking about rewards in heaven—but in a future to which our living will have made its contribution, if only by having really taken place, a contribution which we can will to make when we reflect upon it consciously.

What shall we say about our author's fourth hypothesis [67, 104, 168, 197f., 225, 247, 276] concerning metaphysics (it coincides with the middle of the three layers in the metaphysical cake)—the hypothesis that metaphysical statements are proposals for linguistic change? My suggestion is that, with suitable qualifications, this, too, is acceptable. But here again we must allow for a distinction between good and bad, or balanced and unbalanced, metaphysics. It is rather bad metaphysics to say, "There are no things or persons, but only events." For who can really restrict himself to the language of events? But it may be good metaphysics to argue that *a full analysis* of things and persons must be in the language of events-occurrences, or acts—a language which needs to be carefully developed, not that it may displace ordinary language, but that it may supplement it for philosophical and scientific purposes. Ordinary language is then viewed as perfectly proper and invaluable shorthand, adequate save for certain ultimate purposes, i.e., purposes of understanding the subtler contingent aspects of the world, or the eternal and necessary aspects. Ordinary language is not "self-contradictory," as ordinarily used; but it becomes self-contradictory when pressed too hard for analytic purposes, scientific or metaphysical.

There are, however, certain points where common sense (or what some might call that) and everyday speech do encroach upon metaphysical issues. These are particularly in religious matters, or where some aspect of infinity or perfection is involved. "God" and "immortality," for example, are not literally and correctly expressible in the same terms as most other subjects, unless by the exercise of more care than the plain man has to bestow upon them. So one finds language that is vague or ambiguous and is saved from absurdity only by a sensitive feeling for context—and not entirely even in that way. Thus if a pious man is unfortunate, he may wonder "why God has done this to him"; but if he feels that he has sinned, he does not attribute his sin to God, but to his own choice; and yet the misfortune which he has attributed to God can very well arise from the wicked choice of another man, and this he may well know. To avoid this type of absurdity, careful explication of terms is required. Perhaps (and I hope so) some of this care will eventually effect an improvement in everyday speech; but so far it seems not to have done so. The reason, however, may very well be that technical theology itself has not hitherto been adequately conscious, for the most part, of the gulf between ordinary secular speech and even ordinary religious speech. I am not taking sides with those who draw the conclusion that religious language is necessarily symbolic. I think it can have very important elements of literalness—but only at the price of great care to find the balance between tempting extremes, a better balance than most theologians have succeeded in attaining.

Lazerowitz begins one of his chapters (X) by mentioning what I regard as a piece of fairly good metaphysics, proceeds to comment briefly though eloquently upon it, and then devotes the bulk of the chapter to bad metaphysics (the assertion that physical objects are unreal). Why does he do this? Could it be because his method is adequate only if all metaphysics is bad? The "good" metaphysics is an assertion, quoted by Bradley, that reality is composed throughout of feelings, or the "psychical." The analyst then suggests that this assertion "cannot be maintained in the face of fact." [199]. But I do not know what facts contravene (or could contravene) the meaning which a number of philosophers would give to the assertion—taking it in a sense which makes it independent of certain other features in Bradley's system. The assertion does not forbid such usual judgments as, "Rocks (or trees) do not feel (or are insentient)." What is excluded is a type of statement which might indeed carelessly be supposed equivalent: "There are no feelings in (or necessary to) rocks or trees." Or again, "Rocks and trees are in no manner composed essentially of feelings." This latter mode of statement goes infinitely beyond the first, and I believe, and a good many others have believed, that it overshoots the mark and falls into meaninglessness or self-contradiction.

First, let us see how it goes beyond the harmless, "certain things are insentient." There are at least two senses in which feeling may be in or necessary to something which is not itself sentient. An army is not a sentient individual, but there are no armies without soldiers, who are sentient. Again, a finger does not feel, but there is no normal finger save as part of an organism which does feel. (Also, a finger is a sort of army of cells. It cannot be obvious that cells do not feel.)

Similarly, rocks do not feel, but to deny that feeling is essential to them, is to assert *both* of the following disjunctions: (a) *either* rocks have no idividual constituents (even invisibly small ones), *or* these constituents need not be sentient; *and* (b) *either* it is not necessary to rocks to be constituents of any larger whole (such as the universe) *or* this whole need not be sentient. Now I submit that ordinary ways of thinking cannot reasonably be burdened with far-flung negative speculations of this sort. Ordinary perceptions obviously cannot tell us with any definiteness what imperceptibly small constituents or imperceptibly large wholes are like; yet until we know something about these we know nothing as to the validity of Bradley's statement. Beginning with Leibniz there have been philosophers, a small minority, who have thought more or less clearly about the problem of constituents; and beginning with Fechner there have been those who have called our attention to the problem of larger wholes. The most universally competent scientific mind I have known, Sewall Wright, the geneticist, is convinced that physical reality consists entirely of sentient creatures.[E4] He is a man given to saying neither more nor less than he means. He does not intend to impugn (and he does not impugn) essential modes of speech; he is not a "metaphysician" in Lazerowitz's sense. But he is a man who can keep track of the difference between ordinary macroscopic things and radically smaller, or larger, things. Some of my fellow philosophers cannot (or do not), more's the pity.

But, you may ask, is not the foregoing a discussion of a factual question? Of course, "rocks" and "trees" are empirical, factual entities; in so far, we have been discussing a factual matter. But there is an a priori or metaphysical aspect. The conceivable alternatives to rocks and trees would also be things with or without constituents, and they would or would not require membership in larger wholes, and these constituents and wholes would, or would not, be perceivable or conceivable as without sentience. To decide what is possible here, one must have some notion of what forms perception and conception might conceivably take. We cannot do justice to these topics; but I shall mention one aspect.

In a chapter dealing with "Negative Terms," Lazerowitz takes the problem to be set either by those who declare that "nothing exists," or by those who deny that negative facts can be perceived [181,193]. He explains that this last is a way, not literally correct, of emphasizing the correct point that not-red is no color among others, and not-cheese is no physical entity, along with cheese and apples. But the exciting question at issue here is *not*, can negative facts be perceived, but can purely or *exclusively* negative facts be perceived (or conceived)? Here is the good metaphysical question. When we perceive that a thing is "not red," we do it by perceiving it as having some color, or other positive property, which it could not have and yet be red. Blank nothing is not a datum, as the author correctly notes; but it follows that every verified privation of a property is the observed presence of a positive and incompatible property. If this principle is valid a priori—a piece of good metaphysics—then sweeping consequences can be established by applying it to various topics. For example, "something exists" becomes a priori, since it has no positive alternative. Again, "there is no divine being" asserts a privation, the non-existence of "divinity" What then is the presence, the incompatible property, which excludes divinity from existence? (For, to repeat, either there can be purely negative facts, or all non-existence is exclusion by something positive. Some would say the existence of evil excludes divinity. I have argued elsewhere (as have other philosophers) that this involves an interpretation of "divine power" which is either self-contradictory or meaningless, and that, as some of us define or explicate "divinity" or "divine perfection," power in this absurd sense is not entailed.

If there is no positive property whose instantiation excludes divinity (and I know of none), then *either* purely negative facts are possible, *or* the non-existence of deity is impossible. This does not suffice to prove theism; for one must still refute the positivistic contention that neither the existence nor the contingent nonexistence of deity is conceivable, since the idea itself is confused or self-contradictory. Hence Carnap refused to call himself an atheist. But the argument does suffice to prove that the central theistic question is not factual, but a priori. The game of "refuting" Anselm has been played long enough—why not give heed at last to what he discovered? (Not "existence" in the ordinary contingent sense, but "necessary existence," the status of "pervading all possibility," is the predicate included in perfection.)

Now let us return to the question of physical things and "feeling." Either there can be purely negative facts, or else the absence of feeling means the presence of some incompatible property. What property? Extendedness? To accept this is to imply that feelings are either nowhere, or are each at a point only. Neither view is defensible, so far as I can see. Feelings are somewhere and not in mere points; hence they are in regions. But is this not what "extended" means? Besides, the most positive explanation of extension is due to those philosophers, Peirce being one, who show that feelings have a social structure which is their extendedness. "My neighbor is he with whom I intimately react"; feelings are always more or less consciously social, concerned with neighbors in some broad sense. Moreover, since the different modes of feeling are social or extended in diverse ways, the whole breadth of the concept of extension can, for all anyone has shown, be dealt with in terms of them.

The only properties which do exclude feelings are extremes of disunity, or of monotonous sameness and repetitiveness. For both reasons rocks, and probably trees, do not feel. But there are no facts showing that either reason applies to the minute constituents of these things, or to the universe as a whole, of which they are essentially members. Moreover, it can be argued that this situation would obtain in any possible universe. Non-feeling *could*, it may be suspected, be no more than a matter of level in the part-whole relationship. This is connected with the point we considered in the fourth paragraph of this essay, that any reality must be ordered, but yet with an element of randomness. But any conceivable state of reality will illustrate these aspects. This does not entail that any world will be ideally right, but only that evil, or failure to achieve harmonious, vivid feelings, will be but relative, and thus feeling will be universally applicable (to all individuals, though not to all their aggregates, or all arbitrarily distinguished parts). The familiar query, Are there physical (spatially extended) objects? has distracted attention from the profounder question, Are there (could there be) *merely* physical (wholly concrete yet in every sense mindless) objects?

Lazerowitz holds that the self-contradictory can give rise to no appearance or illusion. Thus if change even seems to occur, it is not inconceivable. I agree, as to change, but because change is presupposed in the idea of its correlative term, fixity or permanence. The one is as clear as the other, for both express the same contrast. But in the idea of "mere matter, devoid of feeling," we have no such clarity; nor does the use of "feeling," or of "sentient," depend upon any contrast to matter, so conceived. It depends rather upon more specific contrasts between wholes or parts not as such sentient, and those which are; also between feelings for many purposes negligible in intensity, and those of usual or unusual vividness. In such vague negative concepts as "mere matter," contradiction may very well be concealed; and if perception seems to illustrate the supposed notion, this might not unnaturally be termed an illusion.

In his final chapter, Lazerowitz attempts to refute the view (which I have been defending) that a priori or logically necessary propositions express what every possible, or as he puts it, theoretical, universe has in common with every other. Is it not significant that he gives as examples, "Every buttercup is in one place only at any one time," "blue is a color," "a flea is an insect." surely buttercups, blue, and fleas are not items in every possible universe! These seem to be illustrations of a kind of indirect empirical truth. In every a priori sentence there is at least *one* empirical element: the fact that certain words happen to have certain meanings. In *some* so-called "a priori" sentences there is an additional empirical element, in that the things for which the words stand are themselves merely empirical or contingent. In "All fleas are insects," what is purely a priori is, of course, only the logical truism that members of a subclass of a class C must be members of C. If in any conceivable state of affairs there must (at least for omniscience) be classifiable items, then this truism is metaphysical. But "blue is a color," for example, is not, since one can, so far at least as I can see, very well conceive of a total reality lacking any such quality as "blue" stands for. Not even "not-blue" (or its verbal equivalent) must have meaning in any possible world; for the question of blue does not arise at all except under special conditions, and all special conditions are contingent. The consideration that such a sentence as "fleas cannot fail to be insects" might be vacuously true, and that indeed there might have been neither fleas nor 'fleas' should not mislead us into supposing that all terms and their referents must similarly be contingent. It turns out, for example, to involve contradiction to treat "deity exists" in this way. The phrase, to be sure, is contingent; but not what it is defined to mean. Here the linguistic factor is the *only* contingent one. There are alternatives to 'the existence of God' but not to the existence of God (assume 'God' has a consistent meaning). Nor, I think, is there any alternative to the existence of some world, some positive state of nondivine reality, or other.

Our author casts delicate ridicule upon the notion that a logical necessity has any analogy to a real or causal necessity, a sort of inflexibility in things which cannot be overcome. But there are many degrees and sorts of analogy, as linguistic analysts know when it comes to language, and often forget when it comes to anything else. The metaphysical or purely a priori necessity refers, indeed, to the ultimate invariant, in the sense of common factor, of reality, present throughout all changes, past or to be anticipated. It is, however, rather an infinite flexibility than a rigid inflexibility. It is really an infinite creative and cognitive power and comprises an unimaginably vast range of possibilities, rather than this or that special impossibility. It forbids nothing and is the alternative to nothing, save nonsense, or what appears to be something but is not, such as unthinkable confusion or unthinkable monotony. We appear, perhaps, to be able to think of a disintegrated reality, a mere chaos, or—at the opposite extreme—of a "perfectly-ordered" reality. Or again, we appear to be able to think of a world of things ordered, though not by any divine orderer. We can also say the words, "mere matter." However, is human language and thought so shot through with distinctness that there is no danger of self-deception here? I think there is danger, plenty of it. We are told that "all of us are able to recognize propositions. . . true by logical necessity" [254]. The obvious and trite ones, yes, but all? I disagree. Clearly these matters are not easy; and Lazerowitz's psychological-linguistic explanation of metaphysical disputes, while I accept it as more or less true, need not be anything like the whole story. One needs a certain ability, and perhaps above all a certain disinterestedness, to explore such questions with the sort of perspicacity and freedom which their clarification requires. Such disinterestedness seems rare (and I rather fancy that even the ability is not so common as some suppose).

Non-theists generally are not very willing to explore the possible formulations of theism in order to find whether or not there is one which makes sense (as some assuredly do not). Theists generally are reluctant to explore, not only forms of atheism, but even the possible formulations, other than their own, of theism. On the contrary, a theist usually becomes attached to one form early in his career, and adheres to it through every turn in his thought, caricaturing alternatives rather than investigating them. There are many reasons for this narrow-minded stubbornness; but how can it prove that there is no truth to discover in such matters? Until we overcome these bad ways of thinking to a greater extent than we yet have, we shall not be in a position to judge! And the fine logicians of our time for the most part only play at thinking about essential philosophical questions; they do not seriously attend to them in an objective, systematic way.

We have centuries of speculation behind us, but possible (if we escape self-destruction) hundreds of millions ahead of us. Metaphysics is not old; it is very young, on such a scale!

One important cause of disagreement among metaphysicians is religious dogma and clerical intolerance. And, partly by natural reaction, anti-clericals and skeptics are possibly just as unfree. We face all the temptations Lazerowitz sees, plus those to which he himself appears to have yielded, and doubtless many more besides. This subject is assuredly in several senses more difficult than arithmetic.

My conclusion is that our author has given us a helpful but truncated analysis of metaphysics, an analysis which is one-sided because it deals chiefly with one-sided or crude examples (never with the subtlest and best balanced ones!), thus giving the incorrect impression that metaphysics, intellectually, can only be one-sided or crude, a perverse tour de force. So it sometimes is.

It is greatly to be hoped that such books as this will stimulate an improvement in our methods of seeking a priori knowledge of the strictly necessary aspects of existence—those common to all conceivable states of reality, though not to all those which, to casual consideration, appear to be conceivable.

HOW SOME SPEAK, YET DO NOT SPEAK, ABOUT GOD

Twenty-five years ago a critic of my ontological argument reminded us that if the premises of the argument are tautological rather than factual, that is, if they are "true in all possible worlds, then. . . they are vacuously true, since they then tell us nothing particular about our world."[E5] He failed to note that by "the existence of God" is not properly intended a "particular" feature of "our" or "the real world," but only a purely *general* status of any world whatever; that if that world exists God created it; and if it does not but could exist, God could create it. Naturally, then, if "God exists" has consistent sense, it is true in any possible world; this is one of the many ways of putting Anselm's point. The divine existence cannot stand or fall with that of a certain world, a certain contingent thing, for that would mean that the creator was a mere creature! God's existence is not, in the proper sense, "particular" at all, though the divine actuality (as we shall see presently) is indeed so.

Professor Zabeeh is right in this: the essential question is whether the idea of God, or that of necessary, uncreated-yet-individual existence makes sense. Anselm frankly assumed that it did. Against the positivistic contention to the contrary a supplementary argument is needed, and here (for reasons we shall hint at presently) Anselm was in trouble. But, with a different philosophy, the supplementary argument can perhaps be provided. And in any case, the Anselmian proof does accomplish something; for it simplifies the question of the truth of theism by making this truth equivalent to the falsity of the positivistic contention that there is no logically possible idea of God. Atheism is at best a confusion; theism or positivism is the choice we have to make. This is a valuable simplification. The atheist discusses the word, not the idea, of "God." Only positivists and theists address themselves to the real question. And the theists must not be pure empiricists; for the existence of deity as an empirical question has no logical standing.

Zabeeh's willingness to beg the question he purported to discuss is breath-taking. Thus, leaning on Hume: "it is a brute fact that every object or impression which exists, *could* cease to exist." Again, leaning on Ryle: "since things do happen to wear out, it is rational to expect them to wither away. . . ." And so the weakness of the creatures is *ohne weiteres* attributable also to the creator! By what rule of logic? Surely it cannot be God who is here referred to!

Professor Zabeeh is right that the mere use of a word cannot establish a necessity. However, as Findlay (and others) has shown, it is the meaning not just of "God" but of the attitude of worship in the high religions that it refers to a not conceivably [by others] surpassable being.[E6] Since no such being could be a contingently existing thing, i.e., a mere creature, either worship is self-contradictory (rather than merely mistaken), or its object exists necessarily.

We are told that "necessity" applies only to propositions. But (a) if the proposition, *divinity exists*, is admitted to be necessary, then Anselm's chief point is granted; further, (b) unconditional necessity, which alone is here in question, cannot apply to a proposition unless it also applies to the thing asserted and vice versa; finally, (c) it is quite possible to define a necessity which is indifferently that of a thing or of a proposition. A necessary proposition, according to C. I. Lewis (whose logic at this point I am prepared to defend), is strictly implied or included in the full meaning of, any proposition, and analogously a necessary thing is one included in, constitutive of, any possible thing. So *universal immanence* in actuality and possibility, hence also in what any well-formed proposition according to an adequate logic implies, is a necessity at once logical and ontological.

The crucial difficulty with the Anselmian proof is, as Findlay lucidly puts it, how could one infer a concrete actuality from an abstract definition? Since the former is always richer in qualities, it could not be deducible from the latter. The less cannot logically contain the more!

The solution lies in seeing that while the existence of God, as not conceivably surpassable, requires that there be a concrete divine reality, it is not itself this reality. By analogy, while "my existence tomorrow" requires that tomorrow I be in some concrete state of thought, perception, etc., it does not imply in just *what* state. Anselm's argument can be rescued from what I call the "Findlay paradox" only if it be conceded that while the bare necessary truth that divinity exists is exceedingly abstract (and only for this reason can it be necessary), the full truth about God is concrete and contingent. An essence exists if and only if it is actualized or concretized *somehow*, in some concrete form; but just *how*, in what concrete form is what I call the "actuality" of the existence (cf. Whitehead's "actual entity"). The latter, the "how" of concrete realization, *never* follows from the essence, even when, as in the divine case, the bare existence, the "somehow" realized, does follow. I submit, for any logician to consider, that: (a) "somehow" is abstract or indefinite compared to a specific description of the how itself; (b) an essence does exist if it is concretized somehow, no matter how. Thus "humanity" exists if there are human beings no matter just which and in what states; and I exist if my identifying personality traits (gene structure, the property, first-born son of—and—, or what you will) are somehow embodied in actual events, no matter which. Upon the legitimacy of applying an analogous distinction to the idea of God depends the possibility of an ontological proof. Most theists have not been in a position to make this application, or to acknowledge the distinction between divine existence and full divine actuality. Classical theism is indeed unable to acknowledge it, but "neoclassical theism" is in a different position. The central difficulty with the proof, the partly unconscious ground of opposition to it, and of the positivistic denial of the concept of God itself, is in the oversimplifications inherent in classical or neoplatonic theism.

I urge upon all philosophers that they give due heed to the manifest difference between *existence*, the mere abstract truth *that* an abstraction is somehow concretely embodied, and the *actuality*, the how, of the embodiment.[E7] The ignoring of this distinction in nearly all discussions of this matter is a marvelous instance of how seven centuries of prolonged controversy, involving almost an entire learned world, can still leave a fairly simple point unnoticed by anyone. It is this possibility of collective blindness which makes intellectual life exciting. There is always a chance of seeing clearly for the first time what implicitly all [or many] have been looking for.

CHAPTER SIX (F)

Religion as Acceptance
of Our Fragmentariness

Religion (at least in its higher forms, and with the problematic, apparent exception of Buddhism) is worship. And what is worship? I offer two definitions: first, worship is loving God with all one's heart and mind and soul and strength; second, it is the acceptance by a person of his or her own fragmentariness. I believe that these two definitions, properly understood, come to the same thing, and that what they imply is the essential truth of religion.

If we love God with all our being, then any love, interest, or devotion which we have must be part of our love for God. We are not, with most of what we are, to love God; and then, with some part that is left over, love wife, child, friend, or neighbor. The very part that is love for another human being must also be love of God. How is this possible? Only in one way, so far as my understanding goes; those we love must be included in the divine Life, in loving which we in principle love all things. God is then to be seen as in some sense the totality of existence. The term 'pantheism'' is ambiguous in this connection, for much depends upon what sort of totality all existence is thought to constitute. The religious view, as I see it, is that God is the one conscious life which includes all lives, without prejudice to their freedom and distinctness. Philosophers usually called ''pantheists,'' e.g., the Stoics or Spinoza, so conceived the divine totality that individual freedom appeared lost. This, however, is not the only way of viewing the divine all-inclusiveness.

Consider now the other definition of worship: acceptance of one's own fragmentariness. Each of us is but a fragment of reality, a fragment in space, in time, in almost any way you please. Our feelings are not the only feelings; for there are at least those of the other animals, human and non-human. Our thoughts are not the only thoughts; for, besides other people's, there are those of the probably vast numbers of other species of thinking animals, which, some biologists and astronomers incline to believe, inhabit the vast universe. And there is the further question of cosmic mind and its thoughts or feelings. In the cosmos we are but passing specks of dust, limited in space, in time, in every way. Religion is what, for good or ill, we do with this fragmentariness, this insignificance relative to the whole of things. If we accept our relative insignificance in the best possible way, we have a sound and good religion; otherwise a poor one or none.

Let us examine some of the poorer ways of facing our situations as but minor items in the vast whole. One way is to refuse to believe that the situation is as it appears to be. Thus we may try to persuade ourselves that limitation in space is of slight importance. "I am small, but is size important, compared to spiritual matters?" What is overlooked here is that size, too, is a spiritual matter. Does anyone believe that something the size of an insect could have the spiritual qualities of a person? And the size of the cosmos means that there is room for millions of kinds of thinking animals, not just the one kind on this planet. Size, like everything else, for a discerning view, has spiritual significance.

We may persuade ourselves that our limitations in time are not what they seem to be. We dream of being immortal in our own right, may even claim to have always existed in some incarnation or other. "I was a king in Babylon/ and you were my Christian slave." Thus one denies the facts of birth and death, explains them away.

I am convinced that we cannot fully achieve true worship until we humbly accept our fragmentary status in time as well as in space. We may talk glibly about "the conquest of space," but as a physicist has said about this phrase, "How conceited can we get?" Any space we ever explore will be vanishingly small compared to the immensities that astronomy knows of. In sober truth, a human individual is but a fragment, neither the whole nor the lord of the whole. The fragment has, it is true, this distinction: it can recognize its relation to the whole. An elephant is also but a fragment, but the elephant presumably does not know this in the sense in which a thinking animal can know it. We human beings are consciously able to accept and even glory in our fragmentariness. This acceptance at its best is worship. Those who do not worship must in some way be forgetting or denying their real situation. This denial takes numerous forms.

There is the person who lives almost solely for that person—as though the whole existed for the fragment. "The world is my oyster"—this Shakespearian pronouncement sums it up. The whole is to serve the part. Does this express our fragmentary status or is it an attempt to deny that status? Surely it is the latter.

There is the person who lives for nothing greater than his or her special group, class, nation, or animal species. To do this is to treat *oneself* as a fragment, to be sure, but not one's group. Yet that too is a fragment. The way we value things shows our real beliefs; to act as though a group within the cosmos could treat the vast whole as mere means to its purposes is to deny in practice what we may verbally say we grant in theory.

Only *one* purpose is an adequate expression of the part-whole situaton in which we stand: the purpose of serving an all-inclusive or divine life. Our ancestors were wont to say that the end of all creation was the "glory of God." Unfortunately, they seldom made it at all clear how our lives could contribute to the divine glory. Indeed, they often declared that God was entirely independent of us in every way, so that nothing we might do could in any way enrich the divine life. This was not the acceptance of fragmentariness, but a subtle way of denying it. We may be but trifling parts of the divine whole, but parts we are; and we must therefore contribute something to the whole. God cannot in *every* way be independent of us.

Besides the exaggerated view of the divine independence just mentioned, there seem to be three chief obstacles in our culture to worship as I have tried to describe it. One is the conventional idea of Providence, an idea which gives rise to the age-old problem of evil, and thereby has been a principal cause of atheism or skepticism for at least twenty-five centuries, probably for much longer. A second obstacle is the conventional idea of "soul." A third is the conviction of many that there are no valid rational arguments for belief in God.

The conventional idea of Providence is that the divine power arranges all things, down to the last detail. To assert this is to open a wide door, on the other side of which lies atheism. For if all is divinely arranged, why are there evils, not only in human life but in all life? Even forgetting the evils, we ought not, I maintain, to view Providence as a power determining the details of existence. According to the idea of Providence, God creates freely; however, as I have repeatedly argued, perfect freedom means supreme capacity to inspire freedom in others. God makes it possible for the creatures to make their own decisions, in such a way, however, that a coherent and in general harmonious world results. Yet the details of what happens in the world must arise from decisions by the creatures themselves. This means, the details come about by chance. For if one creature decides to do X and another to do Y, what results is XY, and *this combination* neither creature has decided. Nor has God decided it. God's decision is Z, and then we have XYZ. Combinations of decisions are never decided, they just happen.

I am convinced that the only world that makes sense religiously is one whose *details* are all, through and through, matters of chance. For not only persons must be free; all creatures down to the atom and farther must have some spark, however slight, of the freedom which in supreme form is divine. If supreme reality is supreme freedom, lesser reality is lesser freedom. It is not no freedom. If this is correct, the man who suffers from cancer should not ask, Why has God done this to me? The cancer cells, or certain atoms or molecules, have done it, not God. [There is also the psychosomatic possibility.]

What then *has* God done? God has done what only God could do, made it possible that a vast variety of free beings should add up to an orderly world. We refer to the basic features of this order as the laws of nature. These laws are indeed God's doing. However, if we take seriously the present trend in science toward viewing natural laws as essentially statistical, we can hold that God determines the laws without having to hold that Divine power determines the details of what happens under the laws. The creatures make their own decisions as to the details. But the laws make it possible for the decisions to result in a genearlly harmonious system.

[God can be conceived to protect creatures in either or both of two ways: by maintaining beneficent laws, or by intervening in particular cases. It is clear that no laws can provide in advance for the detailed needs of partly creative beings. Given the law of gravity, saints and sinners are alike in danger of falling destructively or having things fall destructively upon them. A law that only egregious sinners would suffer in this way would not be a natural law as we know such laws, and would have obvious disadvantages so far as it is useful for creatures to be able to grasp consequences of their actions. A willingness on the part of God to intervene regardless of laws would have similar disadvantages.

But still perhaps the evils in the world are greater than perfect wisdom, power, and goodness would permit creaturely creativity to produce. If so, this fact is either knowable or unknowable. If the former, it must be a nondivine being that could know it. For to suppose God to know it is to suppose God to know himself (herself) to be less than God. On the other hand, how without being divinely wise could one know that the concrete evils of the world are greater than universal creaturely freedom, plus the need for some predictability along with the freedom, could account for? We are not here judging mere categorical relations, as in the classical problem of evil where "omnipotence" (unilateral divine determining of creaturely careers) was to be harmonized with there being any evil at all. Human wisdom suffices to judge that this classical problem is insoluble intrinsically, not just for our powers. But the problem is artificial, since the assumed concept of omnipotence is an absurdity.

I suggest that Hume showed wise restraint when he limited his use of the problem of evil to showing merely that, *assuming the theistic question to be an empirical one,* we are not entitled by the evidence to posit an ideally good and powerful deity, and must strongly suspect that the supreme actual power is either not ideally powerful or not ideally good. But if, as I hold, the question is non-empirical, it follows, as Hume (Philo) granted would follow, that the problem of evil collapses! Within the last two years alone several antireligious books in North America and England have appeared which fail to reckon with this consideration.]

But how, you are probably wondering, can creatures have any freedom of action if they are constituents of the divine life itself? Can a part have any independence of its whole, if the whole is as unified as a conscious experience, with the highest possible mode of integrity, would have to be? Were not the historical pantheists, the Stoics and Spinoza, compelled to deny all creaturely freedom? Indeed, did they not deny divine freedom as well? I reply, they did deny both divine and creaturely freedom in the proper sense of deciding among genuinely possible alternative; but the reason was *not* that they saw the creatures as included in the divine reality. The denial of freedom to the creatures followed from the denial of freedom to the creator, and the reason for both denials was the identification of God with the absolute or immutably perfect, an identification inherited from the Greeks. Spinoza's proof of his necessitarian view takes as premise that God is "absolutely infinite" and immutable. However, freedom in the pregnant sense means self-creation, hence self-enrichment, and it thus flatly contradicts the Greek conception. To be able to act *thus,* and also able to act *otherwise,* is to be able to *be* thus and also to *be* otherwise; for an active being *is,* in part at least, its actions. Each new decision makes one a slightly different being.

Still, you ask, "Can it really be that the supreme form of personal life fails to exercise complete control over its own constituents?" To this I reply, not only so, but any other view is ruled out by the requirements of the problem. To suppose that everything in God is determined by the divine will is to empty the notion of divine volition of all meaning. As Fechner saw more than a hundred years ago, but could not tell the busy or conceited world, volition could not make up the entire content of a consciousness. Action is always and essentially *upon* something, decision is always and essentially *about* something other than just the action or decision itself. Volition gives form to the inner life, but the "matter" which is thus formed cannot be the volition over again. We distinguish in ourselves between impulse and volition; the latter is a sort of umpire with respect to the former. Also we distinguish between volition and perception, we decide what to do *about* what we perceive to be going on. Both impulse and perception in us involve activities in our bodily cells, activities which we do not decide, but accept as material for our decisions. One may blithely deny anything analogous in God, but then why use the term *will* in reference to God? Take away the material on which divine *"will"* acts and all that is left is an empty word.

Here we encounter the famous phrase, *creation ex nihilo.* God deals with no material in deciding; simply God decides, say, that there is to be light, and there is light. I believe that this phrase, *ex nihilo,* supposed to emancipate theology from Greek conceptions, merely confuses the essential issues. I am a creature created by God: am I created out of nothing? If so, then I was not created by using my parents; for they were by no means nothing. Either my parents were genuinely causative of me, or they were not. If they were, then God plus nothing was not the cause; if my parents were *not* part-causes of me, then, by the same reasoning, the creatures are never causes of anything. But in that case, how do we know what we mean by *cause*? We are here reasoning as we did before about freedom: we cannot simply nullify the normal meaning of a term and still use the term as basis for an analogical extrapolation to deity. Whatever the phrase *ex nihilo* is trying to express, it fails to do so in a reasonable and clear way.

If my parents were partly causative of me, then, generalizing this point, in all cases of creation (other than that of a hypothetical first state of creaturely reality) God was supreme, but not sole, cause. The free acts of the creatures, like the activities of our own cells, furnish content for the divine perceptions, so that divine volitions or decisions have something to deal with. Divine freedom reacts to ours. Freedom, merely in a vacuum, is itself a vacuous idea. Freedom is essentially social; it is creative response to the creativity of others. But the others need not be outside oneself. The fact that much of the freedom with which *we* deal is outside our bodies, rather than in them, is precisely because we are not God, not the cosmic consciousness, but localized fragmentary ones. It is odd how the very thinkers who pride themselves most on transcending anthropomorphism are often the very ones who fall into it. Nothing is more anthropomorphic than the idea that to know or influence something is to deal with what is simply outside oneself. To God everything is at least as close and as much a possession (though not a necessity) as our brain cells are to us.

A second obstacle to religion in our time, besides the failure to harmonize creaturely freedom with the divine unity and will, is, I believe, the conventional idea of the soul as something strictly identical at all times, a kind of spiritual container, which possesses all our feelings, thoughts, and experiences, and could go on possessing new thoughts and experiences throughout an infinite future. Elaborate theories of heaven and hell are the natural result. One objection is that if we are to go on living forever, then *in that respect* we are not fragments of reality in time, but are equal to God. By this claim to an immortal soul, we cheat ourselves out of the great lesson which death should teach us, the lesson that a being whose life is limited in time cannot be a final end to itself. The youthful Peirce put this point in an elegant brief paragraph.[F1]

If we give up immortality in the usual sense, the following question arises: When it is all over, what will it matter whether we have been happy or unhappy? To us it will not matter, for we shall not know this having been; but to God it may matter. And if we love God, then it matters to us now. Thus we may care about ourselves because, though perishable, we believe ourselves to be cherished by one who is imperishable. We love ourselves as mortal by participating in God's immortal love. To do this is really to accept fragmentariness. But if we claim immortality for ourselves, then God is needed only as support for our self-fulfillment. I find this blasphemous. Dante's religion is to my mind one of the most sublime of all the forms of irreligion! Ultimately we are but contributory values; God's possession of us is our final achievement, not our possession of God.

Thus belief in a divine life seems the only way to render our fragmentary situation intelligible in terms of purpose. The whole must possess the values of the parts; but only a conscious life, inclusive of all lesser lives, *could* possess the values of these lesser lives. An unconscious whole cannot possess the values of its conscious parts. Only a higher consciousness can contain the world of all inferior consciousnesses. Without the belief in a conscious whole, the conscious parts, such as we are, will be forced to deny in practice, and in terms of purpose, their incurably partial role in the system of things, to pretend that somehow they are more than the fragments which observation shows them to be.

Another reason for belief is the following. The world is ordered, and any world must be ordered. For a mere or absolute chaos is unthinkable. [Relative, partial chaos is thinkable and is compatible with Providence as construed in a metaphysics of freedom. Such relative chaos exists.] But how, or by what, are things ordered? There are in principle only two theories we can form: either things order themselves relative to each other, or there is one superior Something by which all else is ordered. In political analogy, we have either a cosmic democracy, or a cosmic monarchy. There might seem to be other possibilities, such as oligarchy, as it were, rule by a cosmic committee. But within this committee the issue breaks out again: there is either a rule by one, or there is not. *The rule of one, or the rule of many,* this is the final alternative. Now the rule of one solves the problem, and the rule of many does not. Given a supreme directive and a chairman, the members of a committee can cooperatively determine certain details, but with no directive and no chairman, a committee is useless.

It is vain to say, "Let each adapt to all the others." For until there is a general system of adaptation already established, there is no possibility of adaptation. One cannot conform to chaos. So this proposed solution begs the question. But it is quite different to say, "Let all adapt to One and the same supreme Reality." For then a common element is injected into all lesser agents by the one Supreme agent. The laws of nature express this common element. Other laws are conceivable, in effect there has been a choice of just these laws. Can the atoms have made this choice? Surely a supreme creative power must have made it, able by its superiority to gain the acceptance of all lesser powers. It is interesting that a brilliant, and in general rather skeptical, scientist has suggested the idea briefly in a fascinating science-fiction novel, Fred Hoyle's *The Black Cloud*. He writes:

> "I ponder on the existence of a larger-scale intelligence than myself. There is none within the Galaxy, and none within other galaxies so far as I am yet aware. Yet there is strong evidence, I feel, that such an intelligence does play an overwhelming part in our existence. Otherwise how is it decided how matter shall behave? How are your laws of physics determined? Why those laws and no others?"

Worship is the reasonable way to interpret our status as that of pebbles on the cosmic beach, or passing incidents in the great world drama, and yet, for all that, as we cannot help feeling, not without value against the vast background of space and time. We are fragments, but if we are beloved fragments, never to be simply forgotten, that can be enough. To appreciate this, we must stop trying to have it both ways, on the one hand claiming *more* than fragmentary status, as when we assert our immortality, and on the other hand, claiming even *less* than fragmentary status, as when we attribute all choices to God, as though we make none at all ourselves. We cannot reasonably accept the privileges of awareness, and repudiate the freedom that goes with this awareness. But if we are free, then our destinies are in some degree made by ourselves and our fellows, and not by God's decrees alone. Yet our *ultimate* destiny is indeed quite out of our hands in *this* sense that without God a human life would be, as Whitehead puts it, "but a passing whiff of insignificance." In the long run anything human must pass away and be not even a memory, unless God cherishes it forevermore.

Does the freedom of the creatures mean that the divine power is imperfect? Rather, let us say that the perfection of power is shown, not by taking away or preventing the freedom of others, but, on the contrary, by fostering and inspiring that freedom. The creative orator, thinker, artist, inspires creative responses in others; does God do *less* than this? Must not the supreme or perfect artist inspire appropriate degrees of artistic originality in *all* creatures? The price of this view is the acceptance of sufferings, not as divinely sent, but as chance results of the freedom with which God inspires the world. If you want absolute security, total protection against chance, then you do not want to be free in a free world. Indeed, you do not want to exist in an existing world. The price of existence is freedom, and with it chance, risk, luck, both good and bad. Providence is not the alternative to a chancy world: but the power which makes such a world, or *any* world, possible.

God Himself-Herself is exposed to chance, for in caring about the creatures God participates in their good and bad luck. Not even for Him-Her is there absolute security in all that He-She cares about. There is only one way to be in all respects safe: be dead.

I wish now to discuss an historical question. Why has the connection between freedom and chance been so generally missed by theologians? Consider for instance the alleged solution to the riddle of providence and freedom given by Thomism. God causes our acts, said Thomas, but he causes them *as* free acts. And what is it to be free, according to the saint? It is to act *thus* when it was really possible for the agent to have refrained from so acting. Very well, God causes us to act in such and such a manner, but yet so that we might not have acted thus. The only definite and coherent meaning I can, after many years of reflection, extract from this is as follows: God made it possible for the agent to perform, but also possible not to perform, the act. And why was the first possibility realized and not the other? If you answer, because God caused the act to occur, then you are merely contradicting the stipulation that God so acted that the agent really could perform, and also really could refrain from performing, the act. That the act took place was decided by the agent and definitely *not* by God, who merely decided to make a number of alternatives possible for the agent.

Thomists do not follow through with this line of thought. For it implies—what Thomism denies—passivity in God, *divine openness to creaturely influence.* As Jules Lequier, that neglected genius, so well realized: If we decide, and God does not, what our acts shall be, then we and not God decide to that extent what world God is to know.

Freedom is both self-creative and creative of something in all who know the free being. Thus a person, or other creature, as free, is not *mere* creature but also creator, and God as knowing free creatures is not mere creator but also creature. It follows that the distinction between lesser beings and God must be made more subtly than by the flat dichotomy between effect and cause, or derivative and underivative. There is no ground for the notion that higher forms of power tend to give immunity to influence. Man is *much more* open to influence than an atom or an ant; as I have for forty years been in danger of wearying myself and others by repeating. The more sensitive to others a being is, the more power the being has over others. Cause and Effect belong together, and this is even more obvious in higher than in lower organisms.

Another source of the traditional underemphasis upon freedom is the notion of inanimate matter, *devoid of intrinsic spontaneity*. This notion is no longer required, even in physics. Aristotelian theology had no anticipation of this revolution in science. But all theology ought in principle to have anticipated it. Consider: God is love and the creatures ought in their humble way to love God. Love is thus on both sides of the relation. But if supreme love is *supremely* creative, can lesser love be anything but a *humbler* form of creativity? So we have Whitehead's "category of the ultimate," creativity, supreme in God but present in all things.

The flat dualism of matter and mind makes clear-headedness in theology impossible. The myth of absolute inertness as attributed to mere matter keeps contaminating the account given even of the highest creatures. This becomes glaringly obvious in the old analogy of the clay in the hands of the potter. We are not clay, and, moreover, there is and could be no such thing as clay was of old supposed to be, mere inert stuff moved by something else. All creatures have some element of self-motion, hence, by the valid Platonic criterion, some element of "soul," in them. (Aristotle's scandalous denial of self-motion to the soul, based on clever and unsound arguments, was only too influential.) The real source of materialism is in the double blindness which fails to see the self-creativity of experience and the universality of self-determination or spontaneity in all nature. Not only is there an "image" in man of the divine freedom and love; there is a still humbler image of it in an atom.

One main motive in the depreciation of freedom, which goes back at least to Augustine and is also very manifest in Luther and Calvin, is to cut off the possibility of man's supposing that he can save himself, that he can overcome the effects of the "Fall" merely by exerting his will. Perhaps a human being is not "naturally" free to make perfectly right decisons; however, it does not at all follow that the more or less wrong decisions he or she makes are divinely willed. In short I do not see that the special question of grace in human life should be allowed to dictate the answer to the general question, are creatures as such in some degree self-creative? Certainly man cannot choose simply "without God;" for the theistic view is that nothing whatever occurs simply without God. But if the question is, "Does God decide everything and the creature nothing?" or Does the creature decide something and hence God not everything?" then Augustine, Luther, and Calvin gave unclear—or wrong—answers.

We human beings are fragments, but self-creative fragments, and not mere external products, of the higher Creativity. The fragments can deeply enjoy their fragmentary status, all the better if they accept it gladly without self-deception. But this means living consciously for the glory of God, the Inclusive Life, and truly Immortal One, by whom every mortal thing is cherished for whatever beauty and uniqueness it possesses.

CHAPTER SEVEN (G)

Can We Transcend Our Animality?

"Man never knows how anthropomorphic he is."—Goethe
"All the thoughts of a turtle are turtle."—Emerson

Obviously any thinking a human being can do is human thinking. Any thinking a dog can do is doggish thinking. There is, however, one difference. A dog cannot think that it is thinking doggishly; but a human animal can think that he or she is thinking humanly. Every animal is in the prison of its own nature; but only genuinely "thinking" animals can know that this is so. To know a mental limit as such is to be, in some sense and degree, beyond that limit. In what sense and to what degree is the question to be dealt with in this chapter.

We are the animals who survey the animal kingdom and our own place in that kingdom, we survey the vegetable and "inorganic" realms and the place of animals and plants in the general pattern of nature. More than that, we are the animals that see the entire world as an arbitrary instance of possible kinds of world. We can focus on what is not as well as on what is, and on what is remote as well (within limits) as on what is near. We can think of reality or experience in general or as such, rather than simply of this reality or this experience in particular. Because of our great power of generalization, it is easy for us to suppose that we have escaped all anthropomorphic limitations. Yet it seems all too clear, on sober second thought, that this is far from true. The seemingly incurable disagreements among specialists, including the most knowledgeable ones, in nearly every subject of inquiry suffice to show this. Even mathematicians argue about the concept of transfinite multitudes; and in psychology, sociology, politics, metaphysics, religion, and ethics disagreements are pervasive and profound.

Like other animals we have the limitation of perceiving only from a spatio-temporal perspective. We are always here, while most of the world is there, fading away into indistinctness with respect to details farther and farther off in space. Looking at things in the large, even the whole human species is always *here*, with virtually all the rest of the immense universe more or less inscrutably remote and unknown. Even our collective knowledge is from a tiny center of distinctly grasped items out toward a vastness the details of which are mostly beyond our reach. Thus of the millions (or billions) of planets now believed to exist we know in detail but one, and any others that we may add to the list of known and explored planets must, it seems, always be negligible as against the totality. In this respect all animals, simply as such, are severely limited.

The partial inaccessibility of reality to our species is even more obvious in terms of time than of space. Conceive the past as infinite; it follows that the sample of creation's history which we can know is negligibly small. Conceive it as finite, and then it seems fairly clear that we never grasp what is meant by a first stage of creation, a process preceded by no process. All our thinking seems to break down at that point. We would have either an effect of an inconceivable cause, or something which simply transcended the causal idea, and hence our concept for explaining concrete things.

I conclude that concrete reality is only fractionally knowable to such as we are; moreover, it seems impossible to say how small the fraction must be. Of the 8600 or more species of birds (quite apart from the millions of species of other animals) on this planet, none is exhaustively known to any one person, or even to ornithology as a science. And there are the practically infinite possibilities for something like birds on bodies hidden in space. Nor does any man (or woman) fully and distinctly know any other man, or even him (or her) self.

Computers are not going to do away with these limitations. They may change the numerator in the fraction spoken of above; but the denominator is so vast (or even immeasurable) that the fractional character is not essentially altered.

Concrete reality is then, most of it, out of our reach. There remains abstract reality, the first principles of things. Can we not know the laws of nature, beyond any fixed limit? Might we not know something like all the basic laws? Ignoring some of the difficulties which this idea presents, I note one fundamental limitation. If we define law to mean an eternal but quantitatively definite principle of process, it becomes illogical to assert that by empirical inquiry we can have even rough or approximate knowledge of such principles. Samples from a finite stretch of process tell nothing as to what is always and forever the case. Extrapolation of empirical generalizations to infinity does not yield even slight probabilities. It is hard enough (and so far seems to have baffled logicians) to justify induction from short time stretches to very long ones; but this is the most that conceivably could be justified. Experiments show how nature operates now, or at most in our cosmic epoch (Whitehead); but the length of the epoch is problematic; and the jump to infinity is sheer assertion, not knowledge.

Putting the stipulation "independent of time" into our statement of a law is only making a claim, not establishing one. The absence of observed change in nature's general patterns of behavior shows that there is no change large enough to be detected by our means of observation in the time intervals our records cover. But slower changes, for all we can know, remain perfectly possible. Or it remains possible, perhaps, that creation is, in certain abstract respects, at rest for long periods, and then alters abruptly.

Perhaps we could come close to the entire set of abstract patterns or laws obtaining for some long stretch of creation's history. There would remain "the unimaginable past" prior to that stretch, and the "unimaginable future" subsequent to it. If cosmologists really think that by empirical inquiry, properly so-called, they can penetrate these two mysteries, then I suggest that they are dreaming. Perhaps such dreaming does some good, stimulates truly empirical inquiry in useful ways. But this I hold is the most it can do—unless it does one other thing. It might stimulate some to pursue abstract knowledge of a nonempirical sort, the sort sometimes called metaphysical.[G1] This is not the same kind of knowledge as empirical science, extrapolated to infinity. It is not a probability estimate based upon supposedly fair samples. It does not even assert laws, in the same quantitative sense. It is qualitative and assumes no measurements. Its results, if it is successful, do not consist of contingent generalities, such as hold of the world in its present cosmic state, but might fail to hold in some other such state. Rather, metaphysical truths hold, if at all, of all possible world states. Their denial is not merely false but impossible. And the evidence for this cannot be observation in the same sense as is in question in genuinely empirical studies.

An example of a metaphysical truth, according to the claims of some thinkers, is determinism, taken to mean that antecedent conditions and the valid causal laws, whatever they are, fully determine what happens. According to other thinkers, the metaphysical truth is indeterminism, the denial that antecedent conditions and laws fully determine what happens. Either way one is not appealing to measurements which have been or could be made. For all parties, if they have their wits about them, know that we shall never have absolute measurements of antecedent conditions and so can never verify quantitatively, even in a single case, that what happens was, or was not, fully determined by the conditions.

It is important that neither determinist nor indeterminist (simply as such) is attempting to find out how much departure from strict regularity, how much randomness, there is in nature. They are not measuring degrees of disorder. Rather, the determinist (in the strict sense) says that there is none to measure and his opponent that there is some. The issue is between zero and some indeterminate finite quantity. In other words, it is between the acceptance or rejection of a category, and this category is not causality but creation, in a sense to be explicated below.

Zero is a sort of quantity, but with one exception an unobservable one. Only where there is abrupt discontinuity can one observe a pure absence. Thus the zero of elephants in a room is observable because nothing else is much like an elephant, and the smallest elephant is still observably large. But natural laws of the kind required to predict what happens involve continuous variables, e.g., velocity, acceleration, angle of incidence. Observations of values under these variables are at best approximate.

Diverse conclusions have been drawn from this situation. Some infer that the determinism-indeterminism issue is without cognitive meaning, a mere matter of how we wish to talk. Others hold that determinism is a necessary, or at least helpful, postulate of knowledge, though not one of its results. Still others, myself among them, think that a certain qualified indeterminism, or qualified determinism (the qualification, or nonabsoluteness, being the essential point) is a necessary element of any possible knowledge that understands itself.

On the one hand, mere or absolute indeterminism is an extreme that does not make sense. "No matter what has happened up to now, anything may happen next with equal probability"—these words can be uttered, but no animal can act in accordance with what they seem to say. Just to live is to face the future in terms of the past. A sheer lack of causal connectedness is pragmatically unrealizable. We are going, to some extent, to predict the furture and regard it as in some degree already determined. The only live issue is as to the extent of this determination. Is it complete, so that inability to predict is simply ignorance of the past or of valid laws? Or is there an aspect of creative decision in each moment of process, so that what happens is only in more or less abstract outline, not in full concreteness, the one and only possible result of the preceding conditions? Is reality for all future time already fully defined by the (partly unknown) conditions and laws, or is process in each instance an addition to the definiteness, not simply of knowledge but of what exists to be known?

The theory of process as producing *additional definiteness*, creating further specificity, substituting "determinates" for "determinables," may be called *creationism*. Its inventors are Bergson, Peirce, Whitehead, and some others of lesser note. Ortega y Gasset, Dewey, and others have accepted it. It is not an empirical theory. Rather it is an assertion of what every empirical theory ought to have in common with every other. It is thus an elucidation of the very concept of natural law, or of causality as such. (In a fuller discussion the statistical aspect of laws would need consideration.)

The denial that there is any creativity, in the sense explicated above, is not simply the acceptance of an unobservable quantity, zero. A *universal* zero of creativity must be either more, or less, than a particualr quantity of creativity; for it implies that the category of creativity is idle, inapplicable, empty. There are held to be no open possibilities for process to resolve. The very idea of causal possibility is thus implicitly dismissed as vacuous. For determinism, what happens is always in truth the sole possibility; but "sole possibility" is the same as "necessity." And so two distinct modal categories are collapsed into one. (I may seem to be forgetting about "other possible worlds." But I am not forgetting. If real alternatives *within nature* are rejected, the concept of possibility becomes an illicit appeal to the supernatural.) It is not observation that protests against this, but logical analysis. Spinoza showed on a grand scale the paradoxes which result from identifying possibility and necessity. For one thing, not only does the possible collapse into the necessary, but both are the same as the actual. It is not hard to show that with this collapse of conceptual distinctions all other basic polarities become problematic or contradictory.

Let us return to our theme: the human being's capacity to transcend animality. Man (or woman) can transcend merely anthropomorphic limitations, I hold, if he (or she) can grasp certain extremely abstract truths, such as those pertaining to the very idea of law or causality. By contrast, in knowing particular quantitative laws we remain broadly subject to animal limitation; for at most we know the laws of our own cosmic epoch, without any possibility of knowing quantitative laws valid for all process, past or future. But in knowing what must hold of any law whatever we may be able to excape our animality, or status as a localized organism, and know what even God could not transcend. I do not believe that any mind whatever could know unqualified determinism, or unqualified indeterminism, to be true; but I do believe that any cognitive animal that thinks freely and carefully enough will come to the conclusion that causal conditions must, in any possible world, influence but not entirely determine what happens in that world. This capacity to know strictly necessary or universal truth, and thus to transcend the merely animal, is clearly connected with our ability to use language and related forms of symbolism.

The concrete, we have seen, is in large part inaccessible to us, or indeed to any animal. I have so far understated the evidence for this contention. What does it feel like to be a gorilla, a turtle, a bee, an inhabitant of planet X, a paramecium, a plant cell, an atom? We may know what it is like to observe these creatures with human means of observation. But what is it like to *be* them? If there is any content to the idea of God, it should, I hold, include the notion of a form of experience or knowledge for which it is possible to know what each and every creature is like in and for itself. But whether or not God can do this, we clearly cannot. Hence behavioral scientists more and more explicitly renounce the claim to know how animals feel or think.

We can to some extent come to anticipate how creatures will behave, but what their sensations and emotions, their experience rather than ours, may be, this is subject to vague conjecture or extremely abstract reconstruction from their behavior and is for us not even possible content of *adequate* knowledge.

The point is not that we cannot decide between vaguely defined alternatives, such as, do songbirds enjoy their songs or do they not? I believe we can resolve this alternative in favor of the positive assertion. (See the next chapter.) But what we cannot do is have a *distinct* and verified image of what avian enjoyment is qualitatively, in its differences from human enjoyment. We cannot feel bird feelings, but only human ones. We cannot concretely think bird thoughts, in whatever sense birds have thoughts. We can, I maintain, think thoughts remotely like bird thoughts and, with care, reduce the distance between their thoughts and ours. But we can never know just what the remaining gulf between us and another form of life actually is. We cannot even clearly conceive what nonhuman modes of feeling are possible; our language can only vaguely define such possibilities. So it is not a mere question of deciding between hypotheses. The ultimate limitation lies deeper.

But in very abstract matters, language can and does formulate the alternatives. Strict determinism or qualified determinism—one must be right and the other wrong. Inevitably the extent of the qualification more or less escapes us; but the prior question concerns the qualification as such, the validity of the principle of creativity transcending mere causal necessity, so that what happens is always more definite than the range of what was causally possible. Thus it may have been causally necessary, in a certain case, that an explosion should occur; but still the particular forms taken by the explosion, the behavior of each atom, and of each human being affected by the explosion, may have been incompletely determined by the causal past; what actually occurred may have added something to the antecedent necessity, determined what was previously partly indeterminate. Here we do know what the theoretical alternative is, namely creativity or no creativity, either enrichment of the definiteness of reality or no enrichment. We know what the question is, and, if I am not mistaken, we know the answer.

In this knowledge our animality is left behind. The absurdity of a causal determination so complete as to exclude creativity is as relevant to one cosmic epoch as to another. It has nothing to do with any special quality of sensation or emotion. I hold that any deity creating a world can do this only by eliciting inferior or humbler forms of that power of determining the antecedently indeterminate of which divine creating is the eminent but, therefore, not the only form.[G2] *A world is in principle a society of lesser creators.*

A literary expression of this, written for children, is found in Charles Kingsley's *Water Babies,*

> "I heard, ma'am, that you were always making new beasts out of old."
> "So people fancy. But I am not going to trouble myself to make things, my little dear. I sit here and make them make themselves."
> "You are a clever fairy, indeed," thought Tom. And he was right.

That is a grand trick of good old Mother Carey's, and a grand answer, which she has had occasion to make several times to impertinent people.

There is one point to be added to this. In making others make themselves, Mother Carey (or any creative power) must first of all make something in herself. A free decision to influence another in a certain direction is a contingent addition to the decider's own reality. God's fiat, "Let there be a world with such and such general or outline characteristics, the details to be settled by the creatures themselves," is an item in God's consciousness additional to God's eternal essence. Also, God's knowledge of what the creatures make themselves to be is no constituent or necessary consequence of the divine essence. If it were, there would be no freedom or contingency anywhere. Freedom is contingent self-making, and causality is simply the influence of antecedent acts of self-making upon subsequent acts, by either the same or another individual.

It may be hard for the creatures to know how much creativity they have, to what extent they transcend causal conditions and enrich the determinateness of reality. In estimating this we may flatter ourselves grossly. Or we may masochistically demean ourselves by denying that we have any creative options at all. But the principle of creativity, without which the question cannot even be stated, remains transcendent of such secondary issues.

The zero of something presupposes the something. Causal regularities mean not the absence of open possibilities, but their confinement within limits. These limits are like the banks of a river. The banks determine approximately where most of the water will go—let us, to simplify the analogy, ignore evaporation and flood conditions—but it is a very different question how far the banks determine where each drop of water, floating body (or molecule) in the water will go. Bringing the banks closer together reduces the options of the floating entities. To render complete the determination by the banks of the destinies of the floating bodies, one must reduce the gap between banks to zero. But then there would be no water (no creativity) and nothing to determine. This is an image of determinism, as some of us see it. It takes an essentially relative idea, verbally absolutizes it, and thereby deprives it of significance. It changes the subject and is no longer a discussion of causality, the concept, but a world whose meaning has evaporated.

I have taken causality as our sample of the sort of very abstract principle in grasping which we can partly elude our animal limits. I could have taken others. I believe that the idea of God sums up all such ideas. Not that God is merely an abstract entity, but that the divine reality has an abstract aspect which includes all that is abstract to the extreme or metaphysical extent. This abstract aspect of deity we might perhaps succeed in knowing correctly. Insofar, we would share cosmic and eternal truth with God. This need not render us conceited. We would still have but a thinking animal's grasp of the concrete. We can extend that grasp indefinitely farther than can other terrestrial animals. But it still gives us but a vanishingly small fragment of the riches of the cosmos. All we can say is that it may serve our needs—if we are lucky and proceed with care and courage. It leaves us still human animals, not God.

Above all, we remain animals in our inability altogether to transcend selfishness. We can grasp abstractly (though, sadly enough, many of our philosophers and religious teachers have scarcely done even that) the irrationality of making the fortunes of one animal organism in space-time one's final and preferential end. We can, though again far from all reputed sages have accomplished this, realize in principle that love of self is rational only as a special case of love of life, experience, and consciousness in general. But we are over and over again, at least in practice, led to treat altruism as at best a special case or derivative or self-interest. We may talk about loving another ''as oneself,'' but the doing of this is as hard as the saying of it is easy. (If there is no such thing as original sin, there is [and this is an empirical truth] something or other which has at least some of the same results.)

One can know enough to know that one has reason to be humble, not so much because others may be better than oneself as because one is at every moment tempted to betray the only ideal which can withstand all criticism, the ideal of valuing other individuals on the same basis as one values one's self, or of helping others in proportion as one is in a preferred position to help them, and helping oneself only for that very reason. The ideal is not so very hard to state, though many are the brilliant writers who have failed to state it. The greater difficulty is in the realization in one's own concrete case.

In facing the concrete, we are never more than thinking animals, highly gifted ones to be sure. In our abstract thought, however, we can have aspects of identity with deity and can to an indefinite extent conform our concrete awareness and decisions with our abstract superanimal ideals. This is what ethics and religion are all about. It is the capacity for generality which is one with the capacity to employ symbols comparable to linguistic signs that makes us in degree unique and preeminent among earth's creatures and enables us, in one aspect, to have partnership with deity.

CHAPTER EIGHT (H)

Metaphysics Contributes to Ornithology

Philosophers have often been something more than just philosophers. Many have been mathematicians, formal logicians, empirical scientists of note, or theologians; a few have contributed to all these forms of inquiry. Intellectual history also shows that purely metaphysical speculations have sometimes (not always!) had fortunate effects upon the development of empirical science. The Democritean atomic theory of the 5th Century B.C., helpful in the rise of modern science, was a brilliant modification of the Parmenidean doctrine (6th Century B.C.) of *being* as one, indivisible, and unchangeable. Democritus and his teacher Leucippus regarded, not all reality, but each atom as indivisible and unchangeable in its internal being, yet able to occupy successively diverse locations in the "non-being" of space. This view, still apparent in the work of Newton in the 17th and Maxwell in the 19th centuries, was superseded only in the present century.

In my own intellectual work, metaphysics and a branch of empirical science have been the most persistent concerns. The metaphysics was widely different from that of Parmenides, and the branch of science was more narrowly specialized than physics, being a limited part of ethology, or the study of animal behavior. My limited part of this is the study of bird song, or, a little more generally, of the making by nonhuman animals of sounds having objectively some resemblance to those which in the human case are called musical. Perhaps instead of ethology I should say animal psychology, since my interest has included the effort to imagine something of the experiences of the music-making animals; for example, how a singing bird—or Gibbon Ape or Humpback Whale— and its listening mate or territorial rivals may feel about the singing. One could also say that I was doing a kind of zoology, especially ornithology, since birds are the music-making animals (other than human beings) par excellence.

Ornithology is a science to which nonprofessionals have made notable contributions. Eliot Howard, a British business man, established the case for the territorial function of song. At least two other writers had seen the point before; but it was Howard, perhaps unaware of his predecessors (in France, Germany, and Ireland), who in 1920 began to make ornithologists, and through them naturalists in general, aware of the importance, for many kinds of animals, of displays to secure spatial separation for breeding and foraging purposes.[H1] Oddly enough, although some fine ornithologists have been Clergymen, others painters, one a dentist, another a ballet dancer, several physicians, the combination of philosophy and ornithology seems to have been rare. Aristotle, who combined so many subjects, could be named as an early example. Wallace Craig, a student of bird behavior and a founder of ethology, has been classed as a philosopher but seems not to have made original contributions to that subject. H. H. Price, well-known English philosopher, studied problems of bird flight. The fact still seems to be that I am the first since Aristotle to be equally serious about metaphysics—that quintessential branch of philosophy—and ornithology, or that much of it which is relevant to the understanding of the phenomenon of song.

It happened that my experience as philosopher had special features favoring this combination of concerns. In my fourth year as a college teacher I was suddenly asked to teach aesthetics because the instructor in that subject, J. H. Tufts, had been taken ill. This was at the University of Chicago where (in 1928) I was beginning the second lap of my more than fifty-year teaching career. Tufts had emphasized primitive art, especially Amerindian; and I used his slides illustrating this topic. Because of my interest since boyhood in bird song, I began to reflect on the question, "Is not the most primitive art prehuman altogether; for instance the 'dances' and 'songs' of birds, and indeed of some other kinds of animals?" Students of amphibians and certain kinds of insects, for example, speak of the songs of these creatures. I asked myself, "What have all nonhuman music-making creatures in common?" The answer was that all have need to communicate by sound because of inconspicuousness, territoriality, and the absence of any effective alternative means (such as smell) of signalling at a distance. Music-making animals tend to be small and for this or other reasons largely invisible even to mates or territorial rivals; smell is a very minor factor in their lives; and they tend to space themselves well apart from one another. Sound alone can serve their communication needs, and musical patterns are the most distinctive, readily recognized and remembered forms of sound.

Another aspect of my philosophical experience relevant to the study of animal music was my intensive study of the work of A. N. Whitehead. For he, more than any other great philosopher, made aesthetic principles central in his metaphysics. (Peirce, my other favorite philosopher, affirmed this centrality, although his knowledge of aesthetics was too slight to enable him to elaborate the suggestion.) It was Whitehead's idea that all life—indeed all existence—tries to achieve aesthetic value, defined in terms of the intensity and "mutual conformation of the elements of an experience"—the intensity being achieved through contrast or variety, the temporal form of which is the partly unanticipated. Aesthetic failure has two opposite forms. At one extreme we have aesthetic incoherence or disorder and at the other a lifeless, tediously absolute orderliness or regularity. It seemed to me that singing animals produce patterns of sound avoiding these extremes.

The chief question I wanted to answer in these reflections was not, "What in principle is the biological utility of singing because of which natural selection has favored its development in certain species?" I knew and accepted the standard views on this subject. The territorial function I had long known from Howard's book, and the value of song in attracting mates and maintaining pair bonds seemed obvious. But biological utility is a complex and long-term matter. Birds are not zoologists or ornithologists; they build nests, for example, without knowing as we do the function of nests. They may also sing without thinking about the ultimate utility of this activity, as they (and often people) copulate without thinking of the utility of that. Perhaps they sing, at least partly, because they like and enjoy singing and copulate because they like doing that. Evolution selects for activities that help to perpetuate certain genes; but this does not tell us what is in the individual bird's awareness. In selecting for modes of behavior, evolution may indirectly select for modes of feeling that promote such behavior. And so the question, "Is song utilitarian or do animals sing because they feel like singing?" is ill-formed. The two accounts are mutually compatible, but answer different questions.

I knew well the behavioristic drive in all science—a drive curiously ignored by Whitehead, though not by Peirce[H2]—the drive to eliminate from science all self-observed or vicariously imagined feelings or thoughts in favor of the mere bodily behavior, which alone (it is argued) can be intersubjectively observed. However, I have always held that a coherent view of evolution requires us to admit the reality and causal influence not only of human thoughts and feelings as more than mere behavior but also evolutionary anticipations of these far down the scale of creatures, indeed all the way down to atoms and farther. In this "panpsychic" or psychicalistic view I was agreeing not only with Whitehead and Peirce, but with Leibniz (allowing for changes in physics and biology since his time), also Bergson, and many other philosophers and scientists, for example, Sewall Wright, the geneticist, the finest scientific mind I have known intimately. My original reasons for the view were, however, not derived from these writers, but were based on considerations similar to those which led them to adopt it.[H3]

Psychicalism, the monistic alternative to materialism, seems absurd to many sophisticated people, but pre-scientific human beings were inclined to it, as are children; and it is arguable that the alternative doctrines—dualism or materialism—owe their popularity to now largely superseded forms of science. This was Whitehead's view, argued for in considerable detail; Whitehead was also influenced, as was I, by the reading of Wordsworth and Shelley, for whom it was a matter of experience that nature is most directly given as, in Whitehead's phrase, an "ocean of feelings," not as totally insentient stuff or processes. The latter version is not derived from direct intuitions but is an inference rather than a datum. The grounds for the inference are open to challenge.

My work on song did not presuppose the acceptance of the psychicalistic doctrine, but only the admission that the analogy between bird song and human music might help us to discover and interpret facts of bird behavior. And this, if so, would give at least mild confirmation to the view that positing too great a gulf between human and nonhuman forms of existence may impede scientific advance as truly as an incautious anthropomorphism. The song of birds can be seen as a remarkable window into the animal mind, for: (1) it has (in many cases at least) a definite musically analyzable structure, (2) thanks to the tape recorder and other instruments, we have some fairly precise knowledge of this structure, and (3) we also have well-confirmed though of course incomplete knowledge of its biological functions. In addition (4) birds are at once well down the scale in the size of their brains and in limitations in their learning capacities (in comparison to some at least of the mammals) and yet they are remarkably akin, hence intelligible, to us in some of their behavior, for instance in their family life and in their primary reliance on sight and sound rather than smell. Here then is a test case for the behavioristic issue. If we can show the reasonableness of a more than merely physicalistic interpretation of the singing bird, we will have illustrated the value of a more than merely physicalistic view of reality. Our evidence must be from behavior; but our conclusions need not be confirmed to behavior.

For more than twenty years I published almost nothing of my reflections on song. Then in 1953 I decided, encouraged by my wife, to go to school (which I had never done) in ornithology by taking courses for two successive summers at the University of Michigan Biological Station under that admirable and most competent teacher Olin Sewall Pettingill. At the Station there were no other philosophers, only instructors and students in biological subjects, with a basic library in these subjects. I began also attending ornithological meetings, and in 1954 read a paper to the American Ornithological Union. This was published in *The Auk*, the A.O.U. journal.[H4] A number of other essays were published, three in professional journals, others in less specialized media. So I became an ornithologist of sorts.

Although specializing in song, in another sense my bird work was very unspecialized. I was studying, not the songs of this or that region, but of the world. For I wanted to test theories about song as such and to avoid being misled by peculiarities of the singing birds of a particular region. In connection with my professional subject, I made trips, three of them partly financed by Fulbright grants, to lecture (and so far as possible listen to the birds) in Australia, New Zealand, Hawaii, Japan, Taiwan, India, Costa Rica, Mexico, Argentina, England, Germany. some trips wer made simply for bird watching, including those to East Africa and Jamaica. For various reasons I have been, at least for some days, in more than forty states of the U.S.A. and nearly as many of the world's countries. I assembled a collection of tape recordings, some made by myself, and phonograph records of songs around the world and a library of ornithological books. During my many years in Chicago I had the luck to live near the world-famous ornithologist Margaret Morse Nice. There were other helpful ornithologists: Austin Rand, Emmet Blake, etc., in the Field Museum whom I saw now and then. In Austin I had as neighbor for twenty years an extemely knowledgeable expert, the late lamented Edgar Kincaid of *The Bird Life of Texas*. I tried out my ideas on these and other informed people and received much help from them.

After many years of trying to express my theories in *biomusicology* (to employ a term of P. Szöke, the Hungarian expert in the subject) in journal articles, I took the long-contemplated plunge of putting it all in a book. This was *Born to Sing*, which appeared in 1973.[H5] The writing of it took more effort than any of my philosophical works. Although the book is packed with facts, no reviewer cited any definite factual errors (of course there must be some, and I have found one or two); and while some questioned my generalizations or theories, others were sympathetic to them.

The basic theory, which I call "the aesthetic hypothesis," is that songbirds are motivated to sing, at least partly, by an innate capacity to enjoy the making and hearing of musical sounds. They sing a great deal and can hardly be constantly saying to themselves, as it were, "I must sing to warn off territorial intruders or attract and keep a mate," any more—rather less—than human beings make love simply to produce offspring. In both cases sensations or feelings (the former being, as I argued in my first book, a form of the latter) favor the action, make it self-rewarding or self-reinforcing. And this is what "aesthetic" basically means. Songbirds, in short, have a primitive form of musical sense. Evolutionary pressures favor its development in some species because its behavioral expressions make for reproductive success in those species. *A primitive aesthetic musical sense is in some species biologically useful.* Singing by those species is done so much and so well because it is enjoyed as such. In selecting for the behavior, evolution selects for the feeling that activates it.

With this hypothesis I looked at the facts, those already known and those I was the first to observe. I was not solely interested in testing my hypothesis. I hoped by the way to find hitherto unobserved and unexpected correlations, to make significant discoveries about singing behavior. In this I was like any empirical scientist.

My first discovery I called the "monotony threshold." This may be explained as follows. Singing varies in repetitiveness and in degree of discontinuity; some species simply repeat a single brief pattern many hundreds of times a day; others have a repertoire of patterns and avoid repetition of a pattern (or limit it to a few repeats) until they have interposed one or more of their other patterns. The choice of which pattern to sing next in these latter or "versatile" species seems to be largely random. There is no fixed order. Thus the aesthetic requirement of an element of the unexpected is met. But what about the repetitious singers? In the overwhelming majority of cases they act as aesthetic principles require, although not by varying the singing; rather by interposing between successive utterances of their one song time enough for other activities or experiences to occur and for the fading of immediate memory. Monotony in the aesthetic sense, especially in a creature with as short an attention span as a bird, need not arise from singing the same song over and over, provided there be sufficient pauses between utterances. In fact there is a strong correlation of length of pauses between utterances and repetitiousness of the singing. Since my book was published, this has been essentially confirmed by several investigators.[H6] Versatile singers, those with much "immediate variety" (e.g., the Eurasian Skylark), may sing for minutes at a time with scarcely detectable pauses; whereas repetitious singers (many American sparrows and wood warblers, or Eurasian buntings) tend to pause five, ten, fifteen or more seconds.

An admitted and important qualification to this correlation of long pauses with lack of immediate variety is that it seems not to apply to *some* of the many singing species that are not "true songbirds" or oscines (species with highly developed syrinxes or organs for vocalization). This seems to show that some of the physiologically ill-equipped singers (as I call the nonoscines) are also psychologically primitive in their musical sense. Nightjars (e.g., American Whippoor-wills) are the most striking cases of this low level of song development. They do indeed often sing monotonously, and their songs are musically crude or ultrasimple. And so the evolution of muscles for singing tends to accompany the evolution of sensitivity to musical values.

The most striking confirmation of the monotony threshold is in the fact, which I was the first to notice, that in a number of species an individual may sing repetitiously and with suitably long pauses part of the day and at other times (usually in early dawn or in late evening) with some immediate variety and much shorter pauses. Another confirmation is in the tropical Nightingale Wren *Microcerculus marginatus*, some local populations of which sing a long song of dozens of notes each sharply contrasting in pitch with its immediate predecessor and with short pauses (fractions of a second), while other populations sing with no or extremely slight (I was not able to detect them) pitch differences and with pauses at least ten times as long (several seconds) as in the versatile case. A third group sings with variety and pause lengths intermediate between the two extremes. This beautifully agrees with the monotony threshold.

My book records a number of other correlations, some of them complex enough to require a computer to handle conveniently. In a number or respects my book is the first to make extensive use of roughly quantitative methods to test general theories about song behavior. Thus, for instance, I propose a way to measure degrees of singing skill or of song development by the use of six parameters, and show that this skill is correlated with annual amounts of singing (estimated by length of song season and other variables), also with indices of biological need for song, such as territorality and inconspicuousness, thus strongly confirming standard views about the functions of song. (If it cannot be seen yet must influence others, an animal must be heard, and the greater the distince with the whale perhaps several kilometers over which it must announce itself the greater the pressure for distinctiveness in the utterances.) In a circle (or, if it is in a forest, a cylinder) of ten meters in diameter, only one or no species may be calling or singing; in one of 40 meters, perhaps five. And the greater the distance the more difficult is recognition by sight—if indeed the line of sight is not blocked by foliage, rocks, or tree trunks.

A reviewer found the six parameters of singing skill—loudness, continuity, complexity, tonal purity, musical integration, imitation ability—"subjective." He does not mention my own use of this word in the same connection, qualified, however by the negation, "not hopelessly," or my claim that the high correlations with such reasonably objective variables as territoriality, inconspicuousness, syringial development (only true songbirds sing the most developed songs), and amounts of singing per year (song season multiplied by continuity and other relevant variables) show that the admitted subjectivity largely cancels out statistically. Such correlations may be explained away as subjective only if there is reason to view the bias in assigning values under the variables as strongly and systematically favoring the correlations in question. I show that this is highly improbable. In fact the songs I rate as well- or poorly-developed are generally so rated by others who had not thought of the correlations. In one case, that of British songbirds, I use only the ratings of two well-known British writers. My correlations are not disposed of by blanket charges of subjectivity. Nor does it necessarily matter that other writers would assign somewhat different values in particular cases. For instance, whereas my highest ''scores'' (adding the six values for a species) are 48, others might have some of 51 (out of a theoretical perfection of 54, each variable allowing values 1 to 9) or might have none higher than 40. The songs I term superior might still be so, or nearly so, for these others. It is from a list of superior singers around the world, as well as from some lists of poor, or mediocre, singers that my conclusions are drawn. Nor would it necessarily matter if some species I rate as ''nearly superior'' were by others rated as superior, or vice versa. What would upset the correlations would be for some careful observers using clear criteria to rate many of my ''poor'' singers as superior and vice versa. My argument is from extreme cases, not from fine points of difference in ratings.

By 'superior' (rating at least 42) I mean separated from having no song at all by almost as great a difference as a bird is well capable of. If a bird has a single pattern of five notes, that is farther from no song than a pattern of three notes. If the notes are musically refined, as most call notes (expressing alarm or annoyance, say) are not, that, too, is farther from no song than notes that are as noisy as ordinary call notes. The question as I see it is, ''How many small evolutionary steps (transmitted through genes or partly through imitation of elders) were required to get from no song to the song to be rated?'' No one would suppose that a Skylark's, Nightingale's, or Hermit Thrush's song was arrived at in one evolutionary leap. But there are some simple or crude songs that one might almost think of in this way. They are ever so slightly glorified, varied, or refined call notes. The ordinary House Sparrow, *Passer domesticus*, has such a song. It is also gregarious and, because of its habits and habitat, conspicuous. Hence it does not need highly distinctive song.

A special feature of my book is the threefold distinction: call notes, song, and *chatter*. The last is like song in being expecially connected with mating but unlike it in being neither markedly musical nor (in most cases) territorial and in having as primary function that of cementing the pair bond, both sexes working out a pair dialect—in some cases a duet. I claim to be the first to explain in this fashion the imitative ability of parrots, an ability that no one with much biological sense could seriously take to be without function in the wild. I also explain at least one other function of imitative skill, that of increasing variety, hence making high continuity possible without monotony and also contributing to the individual distinctiveness of a singer's repertoire.

In my opinion any success I have had in my venture into ornithology is one more example of how metaphysical principles can help empirical science. They do this by suggesting questions that only empirical tests can answer but that mere observation might not lead one to ask. No one had asked, "Do repetitious singers escape monotony by singing discontinuously, whereas verstile singers sing with maximal continuity?" Nor had anyone distinguished, for this purpose, two forms of versatility, only one of which has much to do with continuity. (A bird may have a considerable repertoire of patterns but sing each pattern may times before shifting to another. The American Song Sparrow, *Melospiza melodia*, sings in this fashion. To avoid monotony, it must and does pause nearly as long as a species with but a single song. Only what I call *"immediate variety"* makes unmonotonous continuity possible.) No one had asked, "Can we measure singing skills, and have they any correlation with amounts of singing per year?" Indeed there had been only one or two efforts to measure these amounts. Other neglected questions were: "Why are parrots so little musical yet so skillful in imitation?" "Why are imitative species in general somewhat less musically exquisite than many highly developed non-imitative singers?" or "How is degree of song development in various families, or smaller groups of species, correlated with the foraging methods and types of habitats of these groups?"

My book thus contains empirical evidence bearing on many previously unasked questions. None of this might have happened had I accepted the widespread belief that aesthetic values are entirely peculiar to our species. I had come to see that cognitive, technological, moral, and religious values are most distinctive of

Homo sapiens, whereas aesthetic principles apply to precognitive and pre-moral experiences as well as to cognitive and moral ones. An infant can be bored by monotony or thrilled by novelty before it can do much by way of thinking and long before it can have a sense of obligation. Subhuman music is a reality, but scarcely subhuman science, ethics, religion, or philosophy.

Methodological behaviorism inhibits investigative imagination in ways not always fortunate. Materialism and dualism (their difference seems, from some points of view, more verbal than real) amount to this: "Do not expect the analogical generalization of variables found in human experience as such (as more than mere behavior) to tell us anything about reality in general." These doctrines "bar the path of inquiry" in certain directions. Birds sing as if aesthetic principles influenced them. I see this, with Whitehead, as illustrating a general rule. Thus Whitehead takes the pervasiveness in nature of wave patterns—a primitive form of aesthetic order, or unity in contrast—to exhibit a similar aesthetic influence even in the inorganic world.

The mixture of predictable and unpredictable that is envisaged in quantum theory is another illustration of aesthetic principles. To have beauty, reality must be neither sheer order nor sheer chaos. And biologists are now reiterating Epicurus of long ago: "chance and necessity" are both pervasive. In spite of Einstein, God does "throw dice." Tedious, unqualified order and hopeless disorder are alike illusions. There is that in the world which excludes both. Neither classical physics nor classical theology understood that order is the limiting, not the exclusion, of chance and caprice. Instead, in both traditions, predictability in principle, predestination, were virtually absolutized and allowed to obscure the reality which is creative freedom, whose actions have necessary but not strictly "sufficient" conditions. Only approximate, abstract, or statistical outlines of the future are causally settled in advance. Too much predictability is as ugly, and at the limit as impossible, as too little. In the singing of versatile singers, for example, it is vain to look for strict causes determining which song will be sung next. The whole point is that the bird itself must decide this. A biologist has defined animal decisions as "unpredictable" acts, in deliberate rejection of the dogma that in principle everything is predictable.[H7] The evolution (in the sense of increase in skill) of song is toward increasing unpredictability—always within limits, since there will be a general style distinctive of the species and, more subtly, of the individual.

The better we come to understand nature, the more, I believe, shall we see that the universal principles are aesthetic. (Is it a mere accident that Einstein and Heisenberg were both musicians and Clerk Maxwell something of a poet?) Since mechanical or absolute order is not aesthetic, we should be pleased to be able to say, with Whitehead, "Disorder is as real as order." Or, in the current jargon, the real order is stochastic. Probabilities are no mere makeshifts to cover our ignorance. They are in principle providential rules for the everlasting game of chance which is existence itself. When Darwin spoke of "chance variations" he was a better naturalist (even a better theologian) than he intended to be, as he showed by explaining "chance" as synonym for our ignorance of causes. It was his hypothesis that chance is unreal that was the fundamental ignorance. The more we learn of causes the less relevant the hypothesis becomes.

Many scientists, from ancient times to the present, have said that they sought the truth because of its beauty; but as to what constitutes beauty they often had a one-sided, oversimple view, identifying it with a total absence of individual caprice or decision-making. Their aesthetics was naive. The Greek worship of circularity, that for a time misled even Kepler, was an example. It takes no great artist to make circles! The cosmic artist does better than that. In our age the tendency is toward the opposite extreme, an undue emphasis on the arbitrary—as in the music of Cage. Extremes are more exciting to argue about than moderate positions. For this too the reasons are aesthetic. Life, existence itself, is an art. Order sets rules for creative action; and the rules themselves must have been created and must be creatively altered in due course lest the universe peter out in deadly routine. The dramatic character of the big bang theory is at least suggestive. Science and metaphysics are once more close together—but on a new level of subtlety and balance.

CHAPTER NINE

Ethical Rights of Non-human Animals

Legal rights are those which, in accordance with laws and constitutions, magistrates and police will defend. Moral rights are those acknowledged by the conscience of the community. By "ethical" rights we can perhaps denote those which sufficiently enlightened, reflective, disinterested, and knowledgeable individuals would support. I shall concentrate on rights in this third or ethical meaning. Do the subhuman creatures have them?

Three great Asiatic religions teach the duty of respecting life in general, at least in its animal forms, and derive the ethical superiority of a vegetarian diet from this duty. Insofar as these religions assume the possibility that the "souls" of subhuman animals may be in some sense identical with those of past or possible future human beings, their ethical justification of vegetarianism is to this extent questionable. (Certain other reasons for vegetarianism, especially economic ones, seem to me stronger.) However, an ethics of reverence for life can be supported and often has been (e.g., by Albert Schweitzer) without reference to the transmigration theory. An ethical position common to Jain, Hindu, and Buddhist sages, Western Humane Societies, Albert Schweitzer, and C. L. Dodgson (author of *Alice in Wonderland*, as well as of a textbook on symbolic logic) must, it seems, represent a considerable degree of the "enlightenment"

117

spoken of above. Let us consider what may be the ultimate basis for this position.

An ethics can appeal to religious convictions, to scientific facts or principles, to a philosophical system, or to some two or all three of these possible rationales. Ideally, the religious, scientific, and philosophical aspects should form a coherent whole. To exhibit such a whole will be my goal and hope.

My religious faith is in a God who takes delight in the creation. Moreover, I hold that the ulitmate value of human life, or of anything else, consists *entirely* in the contribution it makes to the divine life. Whatever importance we, and those we can help or harm, have is without residue measured by and consists in the delight God takes in our existence. Is it likely that God takes no delight whatever in the millions of other living forms on this planet, yet does delight in, derive value from contemplating, the one human species lately emergent on the planet? If such an idea is not sheer anthropomorphic bias, what would be such bias?

Perhaps you say that God takes satisfaction in the other creatures only because they serve the needs of his darling, humanity. The other creatures are good, but instrumentally so only. We alone are good intrinsically. Immanuel Kant so believed. I say that it took great genius to be so fantastically partial, and yet so knowledgeable as Kant was. His God was an extremely moralistic one, interested directly only in creatures capable of ''rational freedom.'' We, who are such creatures, find the nonrational animals more or less fascinating objects of our spontaneous or cultivated sympathy; but God is supposed to look upon them somewhat as an engineer might view parts of an intricate and useful machine of the engineer's own devising. I submit that such a theology is a museum piece, not a doctrine we can take seriously as an option for our own time or the future. God surpasses us, not by the narrower but by the incomparably wider scope of the divine love or sympathy. Our human somewhat qualified anthropomorphism is not matched by an unqualified anthropomorphism in God. Why think of God at all if divinity is but a more extreme version of our own limitation, our own preoccupation with our sort of animal?

Let us look at Kant's argument a moment. He says that only a rational will that acts according to its rationality is intrinsically or unqualifiedly good. But he also admits that human beings so act only imperfectly or incompletely and that only God always and entirely conforms to rational (or supra-rational) requirements. Consequently, only God is unqualifiedly and intrinsically good. If we add to this, as Kant would have refused to do, but I hold ought to have done, the proposition that even the value of a rational animal is entirely contained in the value its existence contributes to the sole unqualifiedly rational or divine life, what we come to is that intrinsic value consists exclusively in what an existent does for God. Kant tried to locate the *Summum Bonum*, meaning the intrinsic value that measures all other values, in rational animals who are both good, that is, rational in their choices, and happy. I say that the *Summum Bonum* is located in God, who is to be loved by creatures "with all their minds and all their hearts and all their strength." And I say that while rational animals make a special contribution to the Summum Bonum, every creature makes some contribution, however humble it may be.

Not only are adult human beings imperfectly rational, human infants are not rational at all (they consult no general principles in their choices). The Kantian value of an infant is purely potential or instrumental: it *may* lead eventually to the existence of a rational animal. The line between the human and the subhuman is crossed in the life of each one of us, if by human one means, actually rational. I think that a person needs to have something more than Kantian ethics to be a good parent. She or he needs an ethics of sympathy broader than sympathy for life on the rational level alone. And the Deity should be supposed vastly less inhibited in sympathies than are human beings. *Life sharing*, delighting in the lives of others, this is my analysis of the most fundamental aspect of "love," whether human or divine. What makes the difference between the two forms of love is the presence or absence of limitations in the scope and quality of the sharing. Only God sympathizes with and takes delight in all the forms of life. As an old mystic had it, "all the forms of being are dear to the infinite being himself." [I regret the male pronoun. Our ancestors gave us a defective language in this respect.] So much for the religious aspect of our problem. That "not a sparrow falls from heaven but your Heavenly Father knoweth," I take to be true, and to mean that there is divine participation, sympathetic delight, in the life of each sparrow. Its importance to God is greater than zero. How much greater?—that very difficult question I shall consider later.

Turn now to the scientific aspect of our question. For contemporary biology our species is one very recent branch of a tree of life billions of years old. Innumerable steps led from the ancient beginnings to our kind of nervous system and brain. We have much in common in neural structure (and this is what counts) with other primates, also with whales and porpoises, and a good deal in common even with wolves, horses, and elephants. Indeed, we have something significant in common with all animals, and even with one-celled plants as well. To ask scientists to suppose that all this development is, in terms of value, mere preparation for ourselves and our human ancestors is to ask them to exchange a sublime and coherent vision for a childishly arbitrary one. Scientists, if religious, will want to think of God as more comprehensive than themselves in appreciating the beauty and intrinsic value of the entire vast creative process. If not religious, they will probably have some vague feeling for nature as a wondrous whole to the beauty of which every species makes its contribution, including humanity as (on this planet) supreme but far from sole example.

Up to this point I have been accusing my opponents (the deniers of rights to the lower animals) of anthropomorphism. In my own philosophy I may perhaps seem to be guilty of that weakness myself. I do hold that a thinking animal, in trying to understand things, is bound to employ analogies between itself and other parts of nature. For, if there are truly general principles in terms of which understanding is possible, the thinking animal itself must illustrate these principles. Charles Peirce spoke of an inevitable "zoomorphic" aspect of all our conceptions. I hold that Plato was well advised to employ the analogy of the "ideal animal" in trying to conceive the created cosmos as a whole. And I believe also that the most significant model we can have even of the simplest parts of the universe, say molecules, atoms, and particles, is that they are the simplest, most primitive cases of that which our own natures illustrate in vastly more complex and highly-evolved forms.

There are several considerations by which this approach may be justified. First of all, whereas we know ourselves in two basic ways, we know most of nature in but one of these ways. We know ourselves by being ourselves, by direct feeling or memory of what it has been like to be human animals. We know other things, at least so far as they are outside our bodies, only by visual, auditory, olfactory, or tactual observation. By such observation we can also examine ourselves and our human fellows. Thus, if we can know what any sample of natural forces is like, *a fortiori* we can know those samples which we ourselves are.

There is a second reason, noted by Whitehead, for taking this closest-to-home sample seriously. It is that in ourselves the positive characteristics of animals generally, and for all we know of creatures at large, are present in highest degree, and therefore in most ummistakable form. For example, if adaptability is a characteristic of organisms at large, it is maximal and most obvious in our species. So are flexibility, differentiation and control of numerous subordinate organs or parts, versatility, originality of behavior, sentience, capacity to learn and remember, and finally degree of consciousness and reasoning power. If we ask an atom whether there is such a thing as adaptability, creativity, sentience, we shall perhaps get no clear answer, unless this: either none at all or very little. But the difference between zero and a finite positive quantity makes *all* the difference when we are seeking the general principles of reality. So we had better start at our own end where attributes are likely to be present in sufficient magnitude or intensity to be unmistakable.

For the two reasons just specified I hold, as did Peirce and Whitehead (also Heidegger), that a cautiously positive form of anthropomorphism, that which attributes to other earthly creatures, neither the duplication, nor the total absence, but lesser degress and more primitive forms, of those properties exhibited in high degree, and more refined or complex forms, in us, is the only rational initial hypothesis for us to form. Primitive hylozoism was perfectly reasonable as a starting point for speculation. Indeed, it was more reasonable than the much later and seemingly so sophisticated model, which still fascinates many scientists, of a world machine whose parts are submachines. Machines occur when animals make them, animals are not given birth to by machines. Moreover, we simply do not, and could not, know that there is such a thing as a "mere machine." In Popper's brilliant metaphor, we do not know that clouds are really clocks, that is, purely mechanical in the behavior of their molecules or atoms, and indeed we do not know that even clocks are purely mechanical in this sense. The natural interpretation of quantum physics implies what Peirce for other reasons surmised, that there is no such thing as a mere machine. Quantum mechanics itself is not very mechanical. A quantum system behaves more like a society than like a clock, as Margenau, Capek, and others have noted.

Although we do not know that there is such a thing as a mere machine, we do know that there are animals, creatures whose actions are at least altogether *as if* they were influenced by feelings, desires, hopes, fears, likes and dislikes, memories and expectations. We know, too, that in animals the principle of spontaneous motion, what Plato called the "self-motion" of soul, is normally apparent, whereas in some machines, as in a resting automobile, all the motion or change seems to be confined to the microscale. Since time itself is but an aspect of change or becoming, that model of reality which offers the best chance of understanding change is to be taken seriously, and that model which makes change a mere riddle is not to be taken seriously. It is an open secret of early Greek materialism that the atom of the materialists had, in itself, no principle of change. It was only a bit of stuff ("being" was the word used) in otherwise empty space ("non-being" or "the void"). Why should such a bit of stuff alter its position in the void? No reason was given. Today most thinkers realize that this will not do. So they take four-dimensional process or becoming, instead of being or substance, as the primitive concept. But what is it that becomes? Energy states? But what are these, apart from the geometrical and numerical patterns which the formulae of physics specify? Shapes of what? Velocities of what?

I will not prolong the argument. My view is that every singular active agent (there are no singular inactive ones, the seemingly inactive being composites whose constituents are active) resembles an animal in having some initiative or freedom in its activity and that this spontaneous movement and change has, as in animals, inner aspects of feeling, memory, and expectation, though the effective scope of the latter functions may in many cases be extremely narrow, perhaps confined to a millionth of a second or less. In short, I hold, with Leibniz, Peirce, Whitehead, and many others, including both philosophers and scientists, that all process is at least sentient, and with some degree, however slight or nonconscious, of memory and expectation. I hold also that where there is feeling there is value in a more than instrumental sense. All nature involves self-enjoyment and contributes thereby to the participatory enjoyment of deity, which contribution is the absolute and final measure of its importance.

In spite of Leibniz's efforts to teach us better, we tend to forget the distinction between active singulars and composites. Science seems to show that the activity in a tree is by its cells, not by the tree as a whole, and that the active agents in rivers or mountains are such entities as molecules, atoms, and still smaller objects. So we need not give up the commonsense view that vegetables, rivers, mountains, and other visible non-animal objects are insentient. It is only their invisibly small constituents that are to be understood finally through a remote analogy to our own inner life and activity.

The still unresolved question obviously is, Which creatures are more and which less important—for certainly importance is a matter of degree. It is clear that an animal cannot live without treating at least some other creatures as less important than itself and its own kind. Either our use of other animals and of plants as food is unethical, or our ethics assumes the greater importance of an individual of our own species than at least some of the nonhuman individuals in nature. I hold that ability to interpret this is a critical test for ethical systems.

A logical requirement of any value system is that it should clarify the idea of no value, or of the value zero. I hold that, as value diminishes, its limit of zero is to be sought, not in a form of existence without value, but in total nonexistence. The zero of feeling, of intrinsic value, and of actuality are one and the same. Take the criterion of integrity or unity, as in the aesthetic maxim, "beauty is unity in variety." With no such unity, there is no experience, no value, and no actuality. But there can be experiences with imperfect unity, as in all experiences of conflict, suffering, bewilderment, confusion. Some experiences are better integrated, internally more harmonious and so better, than others. But variety, too, has a threshold below which experience fails. We experience contrasts, not mere homogeneities. When contrast falls below a certain minimum, we lose consciousness, perhaps go into a dreamless sleep.

There is a subtle relationship between contrast and intensity, and between both of these and value. Failure to achieve any great degree of value may be because there is too little contrast for much intensity or too little intensity for any very strong contrasts; but it may instead be for the quite different reason that the intense contrasts are insufficiently integrated, unified, harmonized. There are cases of unified variety where the degree of intensity and level of complexity in the kinds and instances of variety is so low that the resulting beauty is rather trivial. We often use the word "pretty" for such a case. At the other extreme, where the complexity and intensity is great, we are likely to use the adjective "sublime" rather than beautiful. Where the variety is insufficiently unified, we may, if the intensity and complexity are not too great, experience the situation as "ridiculous," funny;

while if intensity and complexity are great the lack of unity or harmony may be felt as "tragic." Thus, as we saw in chapter I, all the aesthetic values are accommodated.

So far in this essay I have been using aesthetic criteria of value. What about moral criteria? I hold that these are either (1) special aspects or dimensions of the aesthetic, or (2) they specify means indirectly favoring the former. The morally good individual is one who wills to optimize the harmony and intensity of living for all those lives he or she is in a position to affect. (1) In living out such a will to optimal aesthetic value for all, including self, the individual inwardly enjoys certain harmonies from the very fact of this form of volition. Insofar, moral value is also directly, or in itself, an aesthetic value. And there is much evidence that disinterested spectators experience a sense of beauty in observing a genuinely good person. But (2) the moral will is also a potential, probable, and intended source of future aesthetic values for those influenced by the actions. Where this is not the case the goodness is bogus, as indeed, alas, it not seldom is. The allegedly "good" people who make life in general uglier, less harmonious, or more tedious, less zestful and intense, for themselves and others, are insofar not really good. It is a defect of our culture that this is so little realized.

In the light of the foregoing what is the value of the human species compared to the others? Only in this species (in this solar system) is there any appreciable development of the moral dimension of value. (This may be unfair to the dolphins or whales.) Moreover, the purely aesthetic dimensions are not in human nature proportionately reduced to make room for this addition. Quite the contrary. Most birds sing, but their music, while good in its simple kind, is not comparable to human music in complexity and, we may presume, in intensity. All higher animals "communicate," but how extremely limited is such communication compared to that effected by human speech and writing!

The importance of a creature depends partly upon the effects it can have upon other creatures. In instrumental value (for ill, alas, as well as for good), no other animal remotely compares with our species. By this test the incomparable importance of humanity is manifest.

John Cobb makes a helpful suggestion. We tend to think that humanity is important because of the values in each individual person; but we tend to think that one Nightingale or one Hermit Thrush is significant chiefly as a specimen of its species. For one thing, such an animal lives but a few years, if it is lucky enough even to survive its first year; for another, individual differences are rather slight in birds; finally, what consciousness does a bird have of its own identity? To what extent does it make definite conscious plans for the future beyond a few seconds or minutes at most? The death of a bird is in all these respects very different from the death of a man. The other animals know fear, but is it fear of death? This requires a concept.

The significance of the term "murder" depends upon much more than the mere idea of killing a living individual. Predatory animals as such are not murderers. They are merely food gatherers whose food is other animals. But when a human killer strikes he (or she) knows about death and has the idea of his species as one among many, and of fellow human beings with whom he shares that unique communication system called language; he realizes that he too might be killed and knows that if he kills another person his act affects the meaning of existence for an entire social group and conflicts with principles without the observance of which by most people he himself would never have existed. Thus murder is one thing, killing by nonhuman predators is a very different thing; and even human killing of nonhuman animals is far from the same thing. True, there is something in common, and those who condemn hunting can perhaps make a case. But the word murder is not to be used to make this case.

For similar reasons use of the same word for abortion is an intolerable abuse. It changes the whole quality of life for human adults, or even for children, if they know that there are murderers about. It does nothing to an embryo to know, for it could not know, that there are abortionists about. And what is destroyed in abortion is not a "rational animal" actually functioning as such. Any rational behavior attributable to an embryo is far surpassed by the more nearly rational behavior of a chimpanzee or porpoise. The human value of an embryo is essentially potential and future, not actual and present. Such animal functioning as is going on in it is nothing especially exalted, as such things go on this planet.

Of course even the potentiality of a functioning rational animal has its value. But this has to be weighed against the values of the numerous actually functioning ones and the harm that allowing this potentiality to mature may do to these actual values. Suppose the unwanted and badly brought up child turns into a genuine murderer, as may rather easily happen. (There is, to be sure, the option of bearing the infant, but offering it for adoption.) Pearl Buck argued that an aborted embryo might have turned out a genius. Yes, it might, and, with perhaps more probability, it might have interfered with the maturing of some other person of genius; it might itself have become a criminal, or at best a mediocrity. And the world is getting rather too full of people for comfort or even for reasonable safety. In any case the moral question of abortion is one thing and the legal question quite another.

How far is the human animal entitled not only to subordinate the needs of other species to its own but, as it now threatens to do, actually exterminate hundreds, and soon thousands, perhaps hundreds of thousands (counting insects) of species? This is a hard question. If the tiny minority of adults who have the sense, shared between small children and adult nature lovers, of the fascination and beauty of all the forms of life could only be turned into a majority, the question would tend to answer itself. For to a nature lover it takes a lot of convenience to balance a radical diminution of natural beauty. Suppose the more than seven hundred species of birds in this country were reduced to one hundred, and in any one state from two or three hundred or more to two or three dozen, would life remain as interesting? Not for some of us. The lovely prairie grass is gone; every lawn begins to look about like every other. How much monotony do we want? Only a few species of trees flourish in our cities. Our parks lack the rich undergrowth that many species of animals require, and so they are dull places, scarcely better than the tiny backyards of the urban poor.

At least we may be thankful, we nature lovers, that pollution sets prudential limits to the destruction of nature to make room for our artificially expanding populations. (Birth control and scientific hygiene are alike artificial, and until we effectively combine them there can be no genuine "natural law" in the case. What is natural without technology is one thing, what is natural with it is another.)

To say that the human species is more important than other species suggests the question, how *much* more? Can we, even if only in the vaguest way, quantify the answer? One human person is "of more value than many sparrows," but is one person of more value than an entire species of bird? Our intuitions seem less responsive to this question. There are not far from nine thousand species of birds. Which would be a greater loss to the universe, the disappearance of all birds, or premature deaths of nine thousand human beings? One could perhaps consider seriously giving up the remainder of one's life if it would definitely save a threatened species for millennia. But it would be merely silly to risk one's life for a single individual bird, whose life expectancy anyway is probably less than three years.

Perhaps the best we can do with this question of the relative values of ourselves compared to the other animals is the following. We can try to view man and the rest of nature as one ecosystem in which our species is ideally, or so far as possible, complementary, rather than competitive, with the other creatures in the system. To this end we can take zero population growth, or even, eventually and for a time, population decrease, as desirable goals. We can put a burden of proof upon each proposed destruction of wild nature. We can weigh seriously the need for luxuries which use large amounts of energy, such as wasteful modes of transportation that require more and ever more acres of concrete for superhighways and parking lots. We can ask if lawns and parks need be so bare of natural undergrowth or bushes as they now are. We can consider nourishing ourselves more largely by direct use of vegetable food, rather than by the very wasteful method of giving this food to animals whose flesh we ultimately eat. Complete vegetarianism need not be and probably is not the most appropriate solution. But the proportion of the grains, cereals, legumes, and other protein sources now going through the meat industry should not be expected to continue. Present high prices of meat may in the end have done some good in educating the American people concerning the basic economic facts. In many climatic conditions, at least, to consume vegetable matter directly makes far less drain upon the natural ecosystem than to let animals use up most of the energy built up in the vegetation, yielding to us only their carcases for food. For the bulk of the energy will have been dissipated by these animals simply by living for some months or years.

An important part of the needed birth control is of births to pet animals. To supply dog or cat food, whales are slaughtered, and in various ways the variety of nature is threatened. Feral cats and dogs are a danger to many wild species. Artificially transformed and maintained species need also to have artificial limits set ot their reproduction if they are not to be an offence to the inclusive ecosystem. Since we are now too numerous simply to let nature take its way as it would do without us, we ought, in all our important decisions, to take thought as trustees for nature in this solar system.

We have indeed no absolute control over nature, even on this planet, and negligible influence in the universe at large; nevertheless, on this planet we have at least, in military language, almost unlimited "nuisance value." We can wreak havoc upon the other creatures and upon our own kind. Were it not for the second of these two dangers, perhaps little could be done politically to check the first. But the fact, now dawning upon all, that our greedy exploitation can boomerang upon ourselves or our children may in time lead our species to save some substantial portions of the wonderful tapestry of life on the surface of this globe. Yet the change of attitude must come rather rapidly if this is to occur. For the destruction of the nonhuman goes on rapidly indeed.

Acid rain, said to come from British auto or industrial emissions, is destroying forests in Germany. This threatens countless individuals, if not species, of animals. Canada has made similar charges against this country, whose administration has been slow to take them seriously. The threat of climate change from such emissions, causing the land areas of the planet to shrink, seems well-founded. Our descendants are not going to appreciate the problems our appetite for luxuries is preparing for them. We think too much about the money standard of living and too little about what makes life deeply satisfying, such as having loving or friendly relations with others, life purposes that make sense in view of our mortality (our being but fragments of reality in space-time), also a sense of participating in the unimaginably rich display of nonhuman forms of life on this planet.

A civilization that in effect teaches its young to seek artificial states of feeling "high" regardless of what this indulgence will make of one's life as a whole and that of those around one, is certainly in desperate need of repentance. Add the casualness with which the population has so far viewed our government's plans to make sure that we can, as one writer to a newspaper had it, "outgun the Soviets." That the freedom we would achieve in this way would not improbably be a freedom of the dead (first by fire and explosion and then by perpetual winter or poisoned food, air, and water supply, did apparently not occur to this writer. Has it sufficiently occurred to our government?

For largely accidental reasons I long ago gave up owning or driving a car, but during much of my life I have used a bicycle. This is also true of my only child. Bicycling is the most efficient, in energy consumption, of all forms of transportation. The drain it makes upon the ecosystem is as nothing compared to the havoc wrought by the automobile. On the other hand, I make some use of taxis, and have been rather free in my use of the commercial airplane. How far this cancels out my contribution to the ecosystem by not owning a car I do not know. At any rate these are among the questions that lovers of nature who know what the ecological score is will take into account.

There are those who say that, since human beings are radically superior to nonhuman individuals, it is hypocritical or absurd to shed tears over ill treatment of subhuman creatures, while ignoring that of many human beings, as of the poor or the ethnic minorities. This argument seems to be at its strongest if the ill treatment in the subhuman case is indeed only of individuals. But the issue is not so clear if it is a question of species, threatened by wholesale slaughter or habitat destruction. All the higher animals, including people, die eventually, and although species also die in the end, the net result, until civilized humanity emerged, had not been to decrease the beautiful variety of nature. Rather the contrary. But human actions now threaten a drastic decrease in the richness of nature's contrasting forms. Moreover, this impoverishment reduces the options open to human beings themselves. We are the only animals capable of being interested in, finding some use for, taking some delight in, *all* the forms of life. This is why zoos and botanical gardens exist. But wild nature has values that such artificial vessels can never more than very partially contain. Even from the selfish human point of view this is true. Thus one finds some of the famous species of songbirds in zoos; but so crowded together with other species that what one hears from them is a discordant, confused, frustrating blend of noises, nothing remotely like the glorious symphony of distinguishable voices one may hear at daybreak in a forest or wild savannah. And the whales and porpoises, those glorious large-brained creatures, are scarcely adapted at all to anything but life in the open ocean. How these creatures really live is very incompletely understood, and only recently has it become known that at least one species of whale has an elaborate song, in some respects far beyond any bird song. It seems a grim fact that the very century in which we begin to understand the life of the other animals—think how the immense role of territory was generally known only after Eliot Howard published his book on the subject in 1920—is also the century in which the destruction of habitats begins to threaten not dozens but hundreds or thousands of vertebrate species, not to mention much larger numbers of lower orders of creatures, animal and vegetable.

My conclusion is that religion, philosophy, and science are best interpreted as supporting the idea that nonhuman forms of existence have intrinsic as well as instrumental values that we are ethically obligated to try to safeguard as best we can. There is also ground for thinking that indifference to the intrinsic values of the nonhuman is sure to lead to unnecessary losses in the extrinsic values of these other types of creatures for human beings. If we are merely selfish toward our fellow creatures we shall probably, like all merely selfish persons, not do justice even to our own selfish interests.

The problem is one of education. Primitive man had a kind of culture that took the rest of creation into account. Our city populations, and our more and more commercially minded farmers as well, are neither primitive nor scientific naturalists. They (many of them) are, to put it bluntly, uncultured persons, a somewhat new kind of barbarians. What is to be done? In Japan and England radio broadcasting takes bird song and similar topics into account. In the United States we seem in some respects on a lower level in such matters.

Yet we do have our Sierra Club and our Audubon Society. We have our Public Television with its superb nature programs. So those of us who love nature are not without allies and resources in the struggle to discharge our responsibilities as trustees for the life of this solar system.

CHAPTER TEN

The Future of Our Species

Because of the invention of atomic weapons, bringing with them the most extreme danger ever clearly seen as possible in the near future, philosophy and religion face a new cultural challenge. It will not do to deny this on the ground that the number of deaths from the two fission bombs already exploded were far exceeded by those caused in World War II by more traditional weapons. For those first fission bombs were in their harmful effects many orders of magnitude beyond all previous weapons; there are now bombs exceeding the first ones by several orders of magnitude; and as the number of such new weapons also increases by several orders, then, since the surface of the planet is finite and in the relevant sense small, we approach a ghastly possibility of an absolutely no-win situation, from which, at best, only animals below the level of birds and mammals might emerge.

In one sense this is not new, except that now it concerns the near rather than the distant future. Physics and astronomy have for decades been predicting an eventual end to our solar system as capable of sustaining life. Some speculate that our technology might enable us to transcend the limitations of that system by colonizing planets in some other system or systems out among the stars. Aside from this rather desperate way of rescuing hope, what other possibilities are there? One is some form of endless personal continuation of life beyond the individual's death, whether in a new bodily form (reincarnation of one's individuality in another person, or nonhuman animal, being the Asiatic verson of this, and some idea of heaven and a new and indestructible body being the usual Western form), or else a bodiless, purely spiritual form of individual existence. The other idea of individual transcendence of death is an eminent form of what is called social immortality. So long as friends, beings who cherish us as we have actually been, survive, we live on in their awareness of whatever beauty was in our feelings, thoughts, intentions, as well as in whatever practical values our behavior has made possible for them. The idea of God can be defined, in one of many equivalent ways, as that of the transcendent Friend who cherishes *all* that we have actually felt, thought, and done, and forever after enjoys what this has contributed to the Friend's life. When Alfred North Whitehead terms God "the fellow sufferer who understands," he is not indulging in sentimentality. He is stating analogically—the only way we can describe the divine being in its concrete aspects—what his philosophical system definitely implies. God enjoys (and suffers) uniquely adequate "prehensions,"—that is, feelings—of the feelings of all creatures. Our feelings thus become "objective forms of feeling" for the Eminent being, whose subjective forms of feeling are divine evaluations of (or how God sympathizes with or feels) our feelings.

If we carelessly destroy much of the life on this planet, we deprive God of the beauty of that life as it might have been for millennia into the future. We cannot, if we love God, wish this to happen. In any case, however, it is entirely beyond our power to take from God the actual values already achieved by the millions of kinds of earthly creatures up to now. Nothing God has can be taken from God. But the future, even for God, is a set of more or less probable possibilities, not full actualities. The final meaning of life is that we have something to say about which of these possibilities are actualized. This is the form the traditional idea of "serving God" takes in neoclassical metaphysics.

Some will attack this theological idea as an extreme; for it exalts sympathy as we know it into an absolute maximum. However, this line of attack is balanced by the opposite one, that sympathy in even its best form is a weakness that the "all-perfect, self-sufficient, absolute" cannot have. I hold that both these attacks make the same mistake: that of misusing ultimate contrasts by arbitrarily favoring one side, independence rather than dependence, being rather than becoming, or indulging in the opposite favoritism. God may be wholly immutable, independent, and absolute in whatever senses it is good to be so, and uniquely mutable, dependent, and relative in whatever sense capacity to change, dependence, or relativity (as in sensitive sympathy) is an excellence. This is my doctrine of dual transcendence. Whitehead's dipolarity is his version of it.

Divine sympathy is unsurpassable absolutely as unlimited ability to appreciate the world, but it is surpassed in its aesthetic content as new creatures emerge, and are divinely prehended. Thus the life of deity is, in one uniquely excellent sense, unsurpassable even by itself, yet in another no less excellent sense it is self-surpassable. It is not extreme in the bad sense; for its eternal nature *excludes nothing positive*. On the contrary, this is the only eternal nature that could enable a supreme life to endow the lesser lives with permanent and definite value. Indeed, without it, they would not be at all. If this seems absurd to a non-theist, so does "without God" to a theist. Theism and atheism cannot both make coherent sense; so, by definition, are all metaphysical questions. They admit of only one answer that makes sense. Is this an extreme doctrine? No, the extreme is to take *all* questions as metaphysical. Spinoza, followed by Blanshard in our day, either did this or failed to make clear what he meant by seeming to deny contingency altogether.

How long should our species last? Some would say, forever. This is the extreme answer. This alone is not enough to condemn it. I do hold that Something should last forever. For if not, then nothing we do has any eventual importance. But why should this Something be a single species of animal? How about the presumptive species (I believe they exist) on far-off planets? What should last forever is either the universe of stars, planets, their constituents or inhabitants and the "empty" spaces between stars, or something more inclusive or transcendent than even this colossal whole. Theism is one attempt to conceive this supercosmic reality. I for one see no very serious rival to theism in this direction of inquiry.

If our species is not to last forever, then how long? The astronomical estimates of the time before the final failure of our sun to provide our planet with a bearable climate seem ample enough. Whatever our kind of equipment can do should have been sufficiently achieved by that time. Being human is a theme that, like all except the cosmic or supercosmic theme, admits only a finite number of non-trivial variations. The reasoning is the same as we used about personal careers. There is a vital pragmatic need for One theme that is worthy of variations beyond any limit. This is the real infinity of deity. However, the human species as theme is far from having exhausted its finite capacity for significant variations. We know only too well how much better we should be doing with our trusteeship for life on this planet and in this solar system.

Some imaginative applied scientists dream of our so deeply establishing ourselves, first in our solar system and then beyond, that finally nothing *could* put an end to the species. This is assuming, among other things, that the natural laws characterizing our cosmic epoch (Whitehead) are everlasting, or that any change in the laws will favor this plan. I suspect that this is an example of hubris in the Greek sense of dangerous exaltation of human importance in the face of the cosmic powers. We are important but we are also destructive. We demand space around us. It is not just the Malthusian food problem, but the general pollution problem, loss of arable land, good air, and water. One could go on. If we are to survive as a species for even some hundreds or thousands of years, we must do what we as a species have not yet shown we can do, deal sensibly with the population problem. Mere arithmetic can prove that the whole uiverse is not large enough for a continuation of recent population growth for very many millennia. Our technology has so lowered death rates that the birth rates favored by our instincts (formed in pretechnological times) are badly out of balance. A recent essay going carefully into the population problem unfavorably contrasted two extreme views (as though the author had read this book of mine) with a moderate intermediate view. There is a serious problem, the author concluded, but it is not yet so desperate as some have thought. In any case we had better deal with it now by means of some other assumption than that we are about to colonize planets millions of light years away.

Pollution by nuclear explosions is not the only serious kind. Coal and oil by acid rain threaten forests and streams and thus important sources of food and good air and water. Germany has already begun to lose forests, and so has Canada, the one because, it is said, of British and the other of U.S.A. industrial effusions. Then there is the excessive warmth, the greenhouse effect, from the same effusions. Many cities, including New York, may be put under water from this source by the melting of arctic and antarctic ice. Our ancestors met challenges in ways that have made us possible. We will not, by getting high on drugs, do as much as they did for our descendants.

A religion that focusses on life on this planet, not in heaven, seems to some of us needed. But it should focus on the planet, not just on our nation "standing tall." Or is it, alas, for many, standing high? The joke is grim. True, we need to be hopeful about ourselves and our country, but our founders' greatness was not in fundamentalist religion. They (including Lincoln) were religious, but by no means fundamentalists. And they know that religious tolerance was essential for democracy. We need faith, hope, and charity—and the greatest of these is charity, and this includes intellectual charity. We are not Gods, and the belief that we *know* a book that will tell us exactly how God sees our problems is an arrogant claim. In Judaism, in Islam, the book is different, in Hinduism, different again. How conceited can we be? Washington, Jefferson, Franklin, Lincoln, knew no such book and knew that they did not. The great scientists and philosophers of modern times have mostly known this also. When they have been atheists, it was partly because they identified belief in God with belief in some human document written or translated by human brains under the influence of other human writings and other human persons, and not solely under divine influence.

For a fair number of theists, fundamentalists and atheists are both "parts of the problem" more than "parts of the solution." And the fundamentalists seem more numerous. Let them consider this: Do they really know *beyond reasonable doubt* what they affirm? Do they know exactly what in a book, any book, is of human, and what if anything is of wholly divine origin? Many great and learned people have thought this cannot be known by anyone other than God. Are these book worshipers that much more godlike than all those others?

I seem to recall that it is said of Jesus that when someone called him good he said, "Why callest thou me good? God is good." Is this "the word of God?" It is a human word about God. I see it as a good word about God. But there are many such good words about God. Ikhnaton of Egypt said some of them three thousand years ago. He preached the divine love for the creatures. To fully accept this is the whole of my religion. It was the central core of my two splendid parents' religion. It was the same for my favorite philosopher, Whitehead. It is expressed in many books and many religions.

There are other ways of responding to the mystery of life. I wish proponents of these other ways no bad luck. Religious belief is a privilege; it should not be used as a weapon to coerce others with. We thinking animals do what we can with our dangerous degree of thinking power. It could destroy us all. Never has humility about our human condition been more appropriate to the circumstances.

I wish to close with some thoughts for my "fellow Americans." Although in my basic concerns I write for fellow members of the species, it seems certain that for any future I can foresee my readers will be mostly citizens of this country. Partly from having some relatives in two remarkable European countries, Switzerland and Holland, I early came to have in some ways a higher opinion of small than of very large and powerful countries. Also, I have lived more than seven years of my adult life in various countries other than the most powerful—France, Australia, Japan, India, Germany (after its great weakening in each of the world wars), Austria (after World War II), Belgium, and (for shorter visits) England, Italy, and some Latin American countries. From these and other circumstances I have come to agree with (and develop further) what an Austrian economist wrote to expound and defend about the difference between small and unpowerful and large and powerful countries. I cannot recall the name of the author of the book.

The small and weak (SW) countries can hardly be extremely provincial in outlook, for their daily affairs are too obviously dependent on several other countries. In a large and powerful (LP) country citizens tend to be provincial, scarcely speaking more than one language, and taking their national form of life as the standard all should try to live up to. It sometimes seems to me that two of the most provincial countries today are the Russian colossus and the North American colossus, the latter much smaller, but by no means weaker otherwise.

If there is a case for standing tall, there is also a case for not fooling ourselves unduly about our position in the world. Bigness and power do not guarantee goodness or wisdom. They may guarantee importance, but not importance for good only. We see this in the case of Russia. How well do we see it in our own case? How many of our citizens have any idea of how our military and economic powers have treated the peoples of the Philippines, Nicaragua, various other Latin American countries, during the past century or so? Have we sufficiently repented of our imperialism? There has been such a thing, as the peoples concerned know if we do not.

On television we have been having a series about past British imperialism in Kenya. We can easily see the arrogance and the silly misconceptions—the British can see it themselves now. My wife and I encountered some bits of it when we visited Kenya before the independence. It was an Englishman who said, "power always corrupts, absolute power corrupts absolutely." Today everybody knows there can be no absolute power on this planet. Russia has seen to that, taking her cue from us and our invention of nuclear power.

Being a citizen of a superpower, an LP, is a mixed blessing. It makes what happens anywhere in the world seem our concern and almost our responsibility. It also means that any large menace anywhere can easily become a menace to us. Who threatens the Swiss? It is the powerful who are feared and the feared who are hated. Russia is gaining an enormous hold in Ethiopia, and in general in the region through or by which oil for Europe, Japan, and ourselves passes. The Soviets are putting many times the aid into Ethiopia, military not humanitarian aid, that we are. May it not be that if our administration wishes to be militarily strong it needs to curb its fascination with nuclear weapons (whose use is a madman's dream) and put more into conventional weapons whose use, while terrible enough, especially considering the danger of any war turning into a nuclear planetary nullification of the entire human endeavor and much else, might still not be absolutely counter-productive?

We may need to stand tall, but we should stand sober, aware that we are only thinking animals, not gods, and that we are all—we human beings—one species, whose destiny tends to become more and more unified, for ill or for good. Is ours the "best" country? Do we have the lowest proportion of murderers, thieves, wife-batterers, rapists, child-abusers, vicious drug addicts? I have yet to see the statistical evidence for such claims. Or are these unimportant signs of a high or low quality of life? How inspiring ethically are most of our public entertainments? What is the percentage of functionally literate, compared to Japan, Sweden, et al.? Can our legislators avoid corruption by wealthy lobbyists?

When American tourists shy away from terrorism in Europe, but give little heed to the vastly greater dangers of sitting in the front seats of moving cars without seat belts or air bags to save life or limb. Is this a sign of rationality or courage? Or again is the rigid fundamentalism of some considerable numbers of American worshippers of a certain book as literally divine paralleled in such countries as Switzerland, Holland, England? Or is it not more like the fundamentalism of Shiite Islam?

Among the political consequences of fundamentalism are disputes concerning the treatment of evolution in public education. In relating the ideas of divine creation, C, and evolution, E, we have four options. We may (1) accept both, symbolized by CE, we may (2) reject both, symbolized by -C.-E., we may (3) accept only creation C.-E., or (4) only evolution, -C.E. Fundamentalists insist on (3), C.-E. Before Darwin, this was the common position. In the learned world of scholars, including theological scholars, this is now the position of a tiny minority. In my long acquaintance with hundreds, indeed thousands, of scientists, philosophers, theologians, educated persons generally, in many states, countries, and institutions of learning, I have met virtually none who accepted this position. It is fifty years since this was a live issue in academia generally. Another small minority are those who accept, (2), neither evolution nor creation, -C.-E. (Perhaps in Buddhist countries this may be common.) The real issue today is between (4) Godless atheistic evolutionism, -C.E. and (1), theistic evolutionism, CE. The explicitly atheistic form is found chiefly in Russia; the theistic form, in most advanced countries. Which side, in this form of disagreement, do the fundamentalists wish to help? There are Marxist scientists who side with fundamentalism: "God or the scientific view but not both." One feels sorry for children taught that this is the choice: turn your back on God, or on science in its going form. And all because the infallibility of God is by some hopelessly entangled with the infallibility of a book!

In spite of my apprehensions about Reagan's conduct of foreign policy and my deep dislike of his attitude toward the wealthy and his tax cuts for them, I find myself unable, after long effort to do so, to Ortega are despotic rulers, cruel to political opponents, with scant respect for human rights. Ortega impressed me on television rather as Khomeini did (before he left Paris), as a deeply hating fanatic, a misfortune for all who might have to deal with him. I was not mistaken about him, but I would like to be mistaken about Ortega. I understand his resentment of the way my country has been treating his country. I recall that our long record of intervention in Latin America has been a dismal one. Also that an imperative of our dangerous time is to find non-military means of inducing third world countries to attend to the needs of their own people, as the mainland

Chinese are trying to do and even Gorbachev seems inclined to do. The case for promoting civil war in Nicaraugua seems inconvincing.

Sometimes I wonder if any writer has ever done more harm than Karl Marx. In Southeast Asia alone how many millions have been killed in his name, as well as by those opposing his influence! Granted others, including "capitalists," have contributed to these catastrophes. Religious fanatics have often brought ill upon mankind; so have atheistic fanatics. Without a better religion than either of these extremes has to offer, what hope is there?

I end by accentuating the positive. Our political institutions are indeed better than most. The two programs, the public broadcasting radio and television stations, and the really wonderful C-Span non-partisan political cable station—these one can indeed be proud of as truly American and truly good.

There are also the consumer cooperatives, truly democratic economic institutions. Would that they might be more appreciated and developed. We need more Americans like whoever it was that planned and created C-Span, and fewer Americans who measure success by the hundreds of thousands, millions, or billions, of dollars they can call their own. "Hardly shall a rich man enter into the Kingdom of Heaven" is a text I take more seriously than many Christians seem to. (However, the grandfather after whom I am named was rich. He designed railroads and seems to have been a good man.) I like my own middle class income well enough. It is partly good luck that my satisfactions can come from other ways of standing out than crude wealth and that I have never been poor. We need more people who can recognize when they have enough raw power through money and can turn their attention to creating beauty of thought, or of art, or other satisfying forms of life, rather than mere forms of "conspicuous waste," in Thorstein Veblen's pithy phrase. In the founding fathers and Lincoln we have statesmen who indeed shine a light for all to see. We have Emerson, Thoreau, Mark Twain, Robert Frost, Henry James, William James, Charles Peirce, and the Anglo-American A. N. Whitehead.

Let us not forget these magnificent creators of value.

Notes

(Letters denote chapters, A for Chapter One.)

A1 For another version of this diagram see my *Creative Synthesis and Philosophic Method* (SCM and Open Court, 1970; reprinted Lanham, University Press of America, 1983), p. 305. This book will be hereafter referred to as *CS*.

A2 I became aware of the Principle of Contrast from a disciple of Wittgenstein.

A3 On C. S. Peirce's admirable generalization of the idea of nominalism (as denial of the ontological significance of logical distinctions), see Max H. Fisch's ''Peirce's Progress from Nominalism Toward Realism,'' *The Monist*, April 1967.

A4 For the Principle of Polarity see M. R. Cohen's *Preface to Logic* (1944) or his *Studies in Philosophy and Science* (New York: Frederick Unger, 1949; copyright by Henry Holt & Co.), pp. 11–16.

A5 I learned about the group of scientists who espouse what I call psychicalism, the monistic alternative to materialism, from the French philosopher, a psychicalist himself, Raymond Ruyer, in his *La Gnose de Princeton: des savants à la recherche d'une religion*. (Librairie Arthème Fayard, 1974). I acquired the book from a Belgian friend, Jan Van der Veken, who is an example of the Scholar from a small country, fluent in several languages, unprovincial in outlook.

A6   Sir Karl Popper is a dualist in that he rejects reductive materialism or physicalism and also psychicalistic monism. His argument is that with life and mind a new aspect of reality emerges: *problems and problem solving*. He does not claim to prove or disprove definitively any of the three positions. If the most general form of mind is called feeling, there seems no way to prove a total absence of feeling from any portion of nature. As for "problems"—since atoms and particles are not indestructible and physicists speak of half-life laws with regard to them, why can there not be problems of survival even on that level? And the laws in question are statistical and do not exclude individual options. It is worth saying, too, that a psychical monism, unlike a physical one, is not reductionistic. For it does not *lower* 'matter' to the status of mind (in minimalistic forms) but elevates it to that status. Materialism is essentially negative: the idea of *mere* matter as in some cases the concrete reality. Idealism or psychicalism as the third option (besides the opposites, monism and dualism) is essentially positive. Absolute negations are suspect in metaphysics, and the materialism-psychicalism issue is metaphysical, as Popper admits the issue between his realism and positivism is. In both topics the question is conceptual (which doctrine makes sense?), not what are the contingent facts? See *The Philosophy of Karl Popper* (La Salle, ILL.: Open Court, The Library of Living Philosophers, Vol. XIV, Book I, p. 149; Book II, 1074ff. Popper has elsewhere argued that atoms are mindless because they have no memories. However, if memory is shown by the influence of the past and if, as seems correct, causality itself is such an influence, then an absolute zero of memory could not be distinguished from the absence of causality. Surely physics cannot show that. Popper seems here to be assuming a definition of memory that begs the question.

CHAPTER TWO (B)

B1   On what I call Royce's sophistry see Bruce Kuklick's *Josiah Royce: an Intellectual Biography* (Indianapolis and New York:

Bobbs-Merrill, 1972), pp. 149, 192, 235. I agree, however, with Kuklick that Royce was a great and noble person. His writings did much for me in my youth.

B2 On James's failure to distinguish metaphysical truth and utility from empirical, contingent truth or utility see CS pp. 285f. and *Creativity in American Philosophy* (SUNY, 1984), pp. 54-56.

CHAPTER THREE (C)

C1 E. O. Wilson, *On Human Nature*. Harvard University Press, Cambridge, 1978. I regard this as one of the most challenging and richly informative books I have read. I change his "scientific materialism" to "scientific psychicalism" and add the idea of creative freedom as universal to the singular actualities in nature, but his "truly evolutionary explanation of human behavior" is to my liking. Philosophers who take empirical science seriously can find in the book an abundance of suggestions for the importance of current biology, sociology, and anthropology for a philosophical theory of the human condition. Wilson knows the limits of empiricism better than some scientificists, even though, in my view, he has little comprehension of the contribution a metaphysics, careful to recognize its limits, can make to philosophy.

C2 M. L. Weitzman, *The Share Economy: Conquering Stagflation*. Harvard University Press, 1984.

C3 The quotation is from the concluding paragraph of an essay by Rabbi L. A. Olan in a book of essays in his honor: *A Rational Faith*, ed. Jack Bemporad (New York: Ktav Publishing House, 1977). In this book are also essays by Bemporad (who understands neoclassical theology), Schubert Ogden, myself, and a number of others.

CHAPTER FOUR (D)

D1 See my essays "The Acceptance of Death" in *Philosophical Aspects of Thanatology*, Vol. I, pp. 83–87, and "A Philosophy of Death," op. cit., Vol. II, pp. 81–89. Ed. F. M. Hetzler and A. H.

Kutcher. New York: Arno Press, 1978. In the same conference was also read Morris Grossman's "Art and Death," which I admire. It nicely supports my main thesis, though neither of us knew in advance there would be this relationship. See op. cit., Vol. I, 77-81.

D2 A. N. Whitehead, *Adventures of Ideas* (New York: New American Library, 1964) ch. 20.

CHAPTER FIVE (E)

E1 Morris Lazerowitz, *The Structure of Metaphysics*. Foreword by John Wisdom. London: Routledge and Kegan Paul, 1955; New York: Humanities Press. My review of this book, here reprinted with slight changes, was in *Philosophy and Phenomenological Research*, 19, 2 (Dec. 1958), 226-240.

E2 H. Reichenbach, *The Direction of Time*. (Berkeley and Los Angeles, 1956), p. 95.

E3 See Hartshorne and W. L. Reese, *Philosophers Speak of God* (University of Chicago, 1953), pp. 97, 102 (sec. 79).

E4 See the closing paragraphs of Wright's article on "Evolution, Organic," in the *Encyclopedia Britannica* (Chicago, Toronto, London, 1948).

E5 Farhang Zabeeh, "Ontological Argument (hereafter the *OA*) and How and Why Some Speak of God," *Philosophy and Phenomenological Research*, 22, 2 (1961), 206-215. My reply, here reprinted with almost no changes, appeared in the same journal, 23, 2 (Dec. 1962), 274-76.

For a century and a half after Kant's celebrated refutation of the *OA* not much new light was thrown on the subject. I defended the argument in my unpublished dissertation, 1923; in *Man's Vision of God*, 1941 (ch. 9); in an article in the *Philosophical Review*, May, 1944; *The Logic of Perfection* (hereafter *LP*), 1962; *Anselm's Discovery*, 1965; Introduction to *The Writings of Anselm*, 1962; *CS*, 1970, chs. 245-260, 281-284; *Insights and Oversights of Great Thinkers*, 1983, 93-103. In all cases my defence of Anselm was a qualified one. It had to be so since I rejected the form of theism that Anselm used the argument to support. Also I realized all along that, as Leibniz remarked, the argument has to assume that the idea of God makes coherent sense. In *Mind*, 1948, Findlay denied this but agreed with Anselm that religion does require that the divine existence be taken as necessary. In 1960 Norman Malcolm published his "Anselm's Ontological Arguments" (*Philosophical Review*, 1960). As one of my students said to me, Malcolm's distinction between the two arguments was one I had been making in classes (also in print). However it was Malcolm who really woke people up on the subject. I think history should record that Findlay, Malcolm, and I have initiated a new era in considering the modal status of theism. In my chapter in *CS* on "six theistic proofs" (I should have said arguments) I present a radically new way of formulating theistic arguments and hold that no one argument is nearly as cogent as a system of about half a dozen arguments.

In *LP* I offered a formalized version of the *OA*. It assumes a special form of the logic of modality. John Hick and others have claimed that the *OA* depends upon a confusion between modality *de rem* and modality *de dictu*. My reply is that there are definite connections between the two, as asserted by Aristotle, Peirce, and others. In any case the essential point of an *OA*, as I have often stated it informally, especially in *CS*, chs. 12 and 14, is not a mere technicality. It is that to suppose a possible alternative to a being conceived as supreme power is to suppose another and really supreme power that could produce it. We have no way to articulate the idea of contingent existence other than that of creativity. Freedom and possibility belong together. Epicurus believed in free atoms, but also that atoms exist by necessity, and eternally. Why? Because for him freedom was only in changes of location. Add the idea of qualitative freedom, then only supreme individual freedom will exist without alternative and eternally, this staus being entailed by its supremacy. But in concrete qualities it will change—by increase in richness. Apart from modality, from both necessity and contingency, nothing makes sense. There must, theism holds, be one being whose range of potential states, compatible with its self-identity, is coextensive with possibility in general. Its possible change is the measure of all possible change, its actual change the measure of all actual change, its permanence the measure of all permanence. It, and not "man," is "the measure of things."

For what formalization is worth, see Billy Joe Lucas, "The Second Epistemic Way," in *International Journal of Philosophy*, 18; 107–114 (1985). Lucas shows how the idea of a being that is cognitively unsurpassable entails the necessary existence of that being. In his dissertation at the University of Texas in Austin Lucas developed a system of modal logic suitable for such problems.

CHAPTER SIX (F)

F1 See Max H. Fisch et al., ed., *Writings of Charles S. Peirce: A Chronological Edition* (Bloomington, Indiana, 1982), Vol. I, p. 338.

CHAPTER SEVEN (G)

G1 *CS*, ch. 2, "What Metaphysics Is."
G2 *Op. cit.*, ch. 1, "A Philosophy of Shared Creative Experience."

CHAPTER EIGHT (H)

H1 Eliot Howard, *Territory in Bird Life* (London: John Murray, 1920; New York: Atheneum, 1968).
H2 A. W. Burks, ed., *The Collected Papers of Charles Sanders Peirce*, Vol. 7 (Cambridge: Harvard University Press, 1958) par. 7.370. (Vols. 1–6 ed. by Charles Hartshorne and Paul Weiss.)
H3 J. B. Cobb and D. R. Griffin, eds., *Mind in Nature* (Washington: University Press of America, 1977). For a discussion of psychicalism (or panpsychism) see essays in this book by Sewall Wright, Charles Birch, Th. Dobzhansky, W. H. Thorpe, David Bohm, C. Hartshorne.
H4 C. Hartshorne, "The Monotony Threshold in Singing Birds," *The Auk*, 82 (1956) pp. 176–192. See also "The Relation of Bird Song to Music," *Ibis*, (Great Britain), 100, 3 (1958), pp. 421–445.
H5 *Born to Sing: An Interpretation and World Survey of Bird Song* (Bloomington: Indiana University Press, 1973).

H6 C. W. Dobson and R. E. Lemon, "Re-examination of Monotony Threshold/Hypothesis in Bird Song," *Nature*, 257 (1975), pp. 26–28. See my discussion of their results in *The Wilson Bulletin*, 90, No. 1, March, 1978), pp. 154–155. See also D. E. Kroodsma and E. H. Miller, eds., *Acoustic Communication in Birds*, Vol. 1 pp. 197, 225, 234, 248; Vol. 2, pp. 57–59, 70, 76, 81, 140–145, 275, 296, 306, 315, 317, 321, 325, 330.

H7 R. and M. Dawkins, "Decisions and the Uncertainty of Behavior," 45 (1973), pp. 83–103. See also in the same volume, M. C. Baker, "Stochastic Properties of the Foraging Behavior of Six Species of Migratory Shorebirds", especially p. 241.

Index of Persons

149

Index of Topics

153